A Beginner's Faith in Things Unseen

Staying Put: Making a Home in a Restless World
SCOTT RUSSELL SANDERS

The Geography of Childhood: Why Children Need Wild Places
GARY PAUL NABHAN and STEPHEN TRIMBLE

*Family of Earth and Sky: Indigenous Tales of Nature
from around the World*
JOHN ELDER and HERTHA WONG, editors

Writing the Western Landscape
by MARY AUSTIN and JOHN MUIR
ANN H. ZWINGER, editor

A Beginner's Faith
in Things Unseen

John Hay

Beacon Press   Boston

Beacon Press
25 Beacon Street
Boston, Massachusetts 02108-2892

Beacon Press books
are published under the auspices of
the Unitarian Universalist Association of Congregations.

The author and publisher gratefully acknowledge the following publications, in
which earlier versions of the chapters from this book first appeared: "The Way
In," "A Tree and a Star," "Stranded," "Swallows and Swallowtails" in *Orion* and
"A Faire Bay" in *Witness*. Excerpts from Archibald MacLeish, *Land of the Free*
(Harcourt Brace, 1938), excerpted with permission of the estate of Archibald
MacLeish.

99 98 97 96 95   8 7 6 5 4 3 2 1

Text design and title-page art by Margaret M. Wagner
Composition by Wilsted & Taylor

Library of Congress Cataloging-in-Publication Data

Hay, John, 1915–
     A beginner's faith in things unseen / John Hay.
         p.   cm. — (Concord Library)
     ISBN 0-8070-8532-4
     1. Natural history — Outdoor books.   2. Natural history — New England.
     3. Indians of North America.   4. Hay, John, 1915–
     I. Title.   II. Series.
     QH81.H365   1994
     508 — dc20

                                                            94-8410
                                                            CIP

To Gemma Lockhart
and the Great Mystery
of her people

Contents

Acknowledgments

First of all, I would like to thank my editor, Deanne Urmy, of Beacon Press, for her clear-headed patience in reading my manuscript. I am also indebted to my wife, Kristi, as well as my daughter-in-law, Joanne Creerand, for their assistance in reading and typing parts of this book. My introduction to the desert under the guidance of Gary Nabhan was particularly memorable, but above all, I thank the land itself for all the insights it has given me over the course of a lifetime.

A Beginner's Faith in Things Unseen

The Way In

One of my earliest memories is of being escorted up the dark stairwell of my family's summer house in New Hampshire. It was quite dark, since we had only kerosene lamps at the time. When we reached the second floor, the only light was coming in from a window at the end of the hall, but this was enough to illuminate a picture that hung at the head of the stairs. It was a large print by John James Audubon of a small flock of Carolina parakeets, now extinct.

I can hardly describe how profoundly the image of that print in the upstairs hall sank in. Those birds, which I had never seen before, and whose names I was not told, flew in out of a wilderness of becoming, world without end. They were of a depth beyond depth, something inexpressible, but a sense to my waking senses, an opening to a new country. I entered into the dimensions of that picture without question.

That print now hangs on the wall of another house. Although I am still drawn to it, it has lost much of its dimension. I stand outside it; it is almost completely flat. My world has been greatly enlarged in concept and perception, and I enjoy the view from a mountaintop more than I was able to as a child. Exaltation takes practice. My first sight of the print, though, had given a first entry into a wide continent that was all ahead of me. I had then no sense of ecological context, and my undeveloped mind was not capable of abstract reasoning. Audubon's print showed me a window on a rich, unending future. Nobody told me that the Carolina parakeet was extinct, and if they had I would not have understood. That bird lived forever, for all I knew. Extinction did not exist. I leaped instantaneously between the birds and their background of bare limbs and hanging leaves, at one with what I saw. First enchantments outlive all the later judgments we make about the world.

For the adult, mind and external nature seem to stand in opposition to one another, a cause of unending conflict and argument about the nature of reality. The exterior is a realm we mean to dominate and control, yet all the life we bypass or ignore in our favor contains the ruling principles of the earth. "Innovations," wrote Carl Jung, "come from below." We are often deathly afraid of it, but down there is where we originated and begin to see.

Nature is not at an end, and does not stand back and wait on our convenience. All we need to guide us lies behind the common phenomena of the world. All things we think of as poor, useless, or insignificant are just as likely to be our masters as our servants in creation.

In her book, *The Mind and the Eye*, biologist Agnes Farber points out that the quality of living things is not only in a continual state of change, but that each organism "has a borderline aura, shading off from the core of its individuality into the environment." This idea may encourage scientists to look deeper into the multi-dimensional nature of things. The rest of us, who do not like what we seem unable to manage or control, are all too likely to look no further, or to take refuge in facts and numbers. But we are all inheritors of the body of the world.

The child sees with the brightest of eyes not yet encumbered by a lifetime of confusing precepts about what he or she ought, or ought not, to see. A culture that preempts the higher qualities of being for itself alone is in exile from the rest of life. It is said that the human species stands out because of its visual capacity. But sight is a universal property in the world of light, shared by a bewildering array of eyes, each reflecting the worlds they inhabit.

For most of my life, I have lived within range of the sea. Out of it in the springtime comes the alewife, the migratory species that swims inland to spawn in freshwater and then returns to where it came from. The alewife's large, lidless eyes, on both sides of its head, seem to offer messages from a depth I am unable to conceive of. That we may be able to dissect the structural properties of a fish's eyes, and to explore the depths of the ocean, does not mean we know these things. The great, unseen ranges are still beyond us. We have not yet discovered America.

Hanging on the wall of my workroom is a photographic enlargement, given to me by a friend, of the eye of a young sharp-shinned hawk. It is so direct, so fiercely bright, that it has disturbed some of my visitors. It has a green iris and a black pupil, and looks like a concentrated whirlpool, circled around by feathers flaring in a wind.

In the hawk's eye is an original, cosmic world we have yet to understand. It has what William Blake, in his poem about the tiger, calls a "fearful symmetry." But this is also the eye of a child.

Follow it, and we might find what we are looking for. We cannot manufacture life. We are unable to see things through, toward rule or ruin, on our own. We are governed by the engines of the sun.

A Tree and a Star

Each morning, the window opened up on a whole sky I had never seen before. Then all the light of day was commanded by the sun. On rare nights, at bedtime, my father urged me out instead to look up at the stars. They were flinging out above the lake and the mountain facing our house like showers of sparks from burning brands. When I was a boy, it was not the distance of the stars that impressed me, but their presence. While they were light-years out of reach, I could meet them with my two eyes. Did this not mean I was immortal? Knowing no more than the familiar universe into which I was born, I had no concept of empty space. If, as I was told in school, there was a limit to the universe, what could there be beyond the beyond, but a nothingness. And that was too much for my mind to grasp.

Every evening, my mother would pull the curtains across the library window with an air of finality that troubled me. I had no idea what sense of tragedy or personal disappointment was behind that gesture. Perhaps she meant to protect our home from a wilder darkness now gathering around us. We try to rid ourselves of fear by lighting the lamps, and now our substitutes for the moon and stars cover the planet.

Still, high above us roam those great constellations in which light seems both fixed and eternally free.

Born into the neighborhood of the universe, it is not hard for a child to believe in transformations. The sparks sent into the air by a bonfire in the wind, or shot into the air by rockets on the Fourth of July, might explain how the stars came to be there, light to light.

I learned how to recognize the Big and the Little Dipper, and Orion's Belt. I also began to pick up some of the old names such as Sagittarius, the great Archer, as well as Capricorn the Goat, Pisces the Fish, and Cancer the Crab. Early in the winter, when light snow lay on the ground, I saw tracks, either of the snowshoe hare, porcupine, fox, or deer. They were winding through the trees, perhaps with an Indian hunter following silently behind them, and they led out across the fields. It was not hard to imagine that these tracks could follow out toward all the others in the sky. In that Sky World, the ancient hunters are perpetually on the move. So the constellation of the Great Bear is explained, in this lovely myth of the Musquakie, or Fox Indians, part of the Algonkian-speaking tribes that were driven westward by the whites.

> They say that once, a long time ago, it was early winter. It had snowed the night before, and the first snow still lay fresh on the ground. Three young men went out to hunt at first light, early in the morning. One of them took his little dog, named Hold Tight, with him.
>
> They went along the river and up into the woods, and came to a place on the side of a hill where the shrubs and bushes grew low and thick. Here, winding among the bushes, the hunters found a trail, and they followed it. The path led them to a cave in the hillside. They had found a bear's den.

"Which of us shall go in and drive the bear out?" the hunters asked each other.

At last the oldest said, "I will go."

The oldest hunter crawled into the bear's den, and with his bow he poked the bear to drive him out. "He's coming! He's coming!" the man in the cave called to his companions.

The bear broke away from his tormentor, and out of the cave. The hunters followed him.

"Look!" the youngest hunter cried. "See how fast he's going! Away to the north, the place from whence comes the cold, that's where he's going!"

The hunter ran away to the north, to turn the bear and drive him back to the others.

"Look out!" shouted the middle hunter. "He's going to the west, to the place where the sun falls down. Hurry, brothers! That's the way he's going."

He and his little dog ran as fast as they could to the west, to turn back the bear.

As the hunters ran after the bear, the oldest one looked down. "Oh," he shouted, "there is Grandmother Earth below us. He's leading us into the sky! Brothers, let us turn back before it is too late."

But it was already too late; the sky bear had led them too high. At last the hunters caught up with the bear and killed him. The men piled up maple and sumac branches, and on the pile of boughs they butchered the bear. That is why those trees turn blood-red in the fall.

Then the hunters stood up. All together they lifted the bear's head and threw it away to the east. Now, in early morning, in the winter, a group of stars in the shape of the bear's head will appear low on the horizon in the east just before daybreak.

Next, the hunters threw the bear's backbone away to the

north. At midnight, in the middle of winter, if you look north you will see the bear's backbone there, outlined in stars.

At any time of the year, if you look at the sky, you can see four bright stars in a square, and behind them three big bright stars and one tiny dim one. The square of stars is the bear, the three running ones behind him are the hunters, and the little one, that you can hardly see, is the little dog named Hold Tight.

Those eight stars move around and around in the sky together all year long. They never go to rest, like some of the other stars. Until the hunters catch up with the bear, they and the little dog can never rest.*

Fireflies dancing over the grass, magic spiders, eagles and buffalo in the clouds, all made the world run with the spirit. Some of the local turtles that delighted me had yellow spots on their dark shells, like the stars at night. One year, it was reported that a black bear had come out of the woods to raid a neighbor's apple orchard. I did not think of it then as a marauder out of the wild, or a "varmint," as the farmers called them. That bear was the intimate of a space I never wanted to lose, a greater homeland whose fires were never put out.

I was told that there were still a few wolves in the hills. I think I was being teased, but I liked to believe it all the same. I imagined them loping silently between the trunks and splintered branches of a wood of spruce trees that grew on a hillside above us. It was years later before we acquired a radio, and there was no television in those days. I met wolves through folktales and myth, and I followed the forest

---

*From Franz Boas, *Handbook of American Indian Languages*, 1911. Reprinted in Alice Marriott and Carol K. Rachlan, *American Indian Mythology*, 1968.

dwellers who had come before us in *The Deerslayer* and *The Last of the Mohicans*.

In our region, of course, there were very few original natives left. Two quiet Indians, a man and his wife, dressed in plain country clothes, came around to the back door in the summertime to sell us toy birchbark canoes and sweet-grass baskets. That these two might be the last of the cast-off forest dwellers of New Hampshire never occurred to me as a child. But they seemed to bring a background of indestructible shadows with them. The white birch bark they fashioned into canoes lay in deep with an unconquerable past. After a few years, these people no longer came to the door, slipping away, perhaps, between the trees.

The names of Indian tribes such as Arapaho, Cheyenne, Sioux, Kiowa, or Comanche sounded beautiful to me, resonant and proud. They confirmed my growing sense of a great continent with a magical, ceremonious past. In our front hall, along with a mounted Snowy Owl, there was a picture of the Grass Dance of the Sioux, with riders on blue horses on the fringe, the dancers at the center. It had been given to a great-uncle of ours by a Sioux chief, who had drawn it while he was in jail. Years later, it was given to a museum, and perhaps a public institution is a better custodian of such art than a family to whom its message is no longer real. But for me, both the owl and the picture meant the presence of a mysterious reality that I would never have known otherwise. When they disappeared, it was as if I had to go on looking for them, even if it took me as far as the stars.

The Native Americans and the wolves were gone, but we were never without the company of the trees. How could we have known where we were without them? No matter how many were cut down, they kept crowding back in, and those left to stand seemed to insist on their right to be there. In their silent way, they crossed the centuries, reaching for the sky.

I remember camping out on a small island in the lake. We ate freshly caught bass by the campfire. When darkness fell, a shooting star streaked across the sky. I was told of an ancient belief that it was the soul of someone who had just died. We slept under blankets on the ground. Waking up at first light, I saw a fiery red squirrel scolding me from the top of a pine tree, like a little masthead of the dawn.

The trees marched up the hills and moved into abandoned pastures, claiming ancient rights of possession. The white pines, with their long, glistening needles, would swing in limber rhythms with the wind. The heavy boughs of the hemlocks dipped their dark shadows toward the ground and lifted up again. Bordering the lake, where thrushes sang in the evening, the leaves of white birch, gray beech, and maple stirred and danced in the breeze. Varying airs pushed small ripples across the lake causing its surfaces to flash in the sunlight. In sandy shallows close to shore, the sunfish circled, waved their fins, and laid their eggs. Farther out in the waters of that sun- and star-crossed lake were the black or big-mouth bass, like ambient shadows.

When autumn came, the maple and sumac of the Great Sky Bear turned red, yellow, and orange. Free winds flung their falling leaves out across the blue sky, where they dipped and sailed like swallows. The evergreens, which were to stand before the winter storms, shedding the hissing snow from their boughs, caught the turning light and were the custodians of the dark. I sensed that these woodlands held secrets from the beginning of the world which would never be uncovered.

Yet the trees were as real to me as my own senses. I smelled the sweet scent of pine needles every day. I built a tree house, really a platform made of white pine boards, nailed to a white pine, and I rode it as if it were a ship at sea, feeling the tree's gentle, muscular rocking in my arms. Wind and trees together sent me ahead on many voyages.

My father first challenged me to chew the gummy resin of the spruce. This required perseverance on the part of the chewer, who had to spit out a great deal of debris before reducing the hardened sap to a pale pink gum that had no sugary sweetness in it at all. The sweetness was in the achievement.

The trees led us out and in, guiding our trails, sometimes sending us aloft like the birds, providing us with firewood and shade. When the moonlight shone through them, or when the sunlight fired them by day, they seemed, in their endless exposure and endurance, to have reached an understanding with the universe.

I was sent to school in the country, starting when I was ten, but my family lived in the city and I returned to the city during school vacations. The only trees there, outside of Central Park, were surrounded by iron grilles, where leashed dogs were encouraged to relieve themselves. The forest spaces were replaced by a tremendous, lighted Manhattan island, which I came to think of later on as a kind of spaceship in itself. It was unparalleled in power and sound. The streets constantly pounded and jarred with their traffic. Trash barrels tumbled and crashed; sirens screamed in the night; the riveting, thundering, and crashing of buildings being erected or torn down was almost constant. Kids shouted and played ball in empty lots, while people talked big money on the avenues. On the far side of the East River, there was a huge, illuminated sign for Sunkist oranges that seemed to rival the setting sun.

As an adult, spending summer days and nights in the city, I walked down streets where people hung their clothes over fire escape railings, and slept out on the open landings at night. When the great urban hive heated up like a giant frying pan, children turned on the fire hydrants to cool themselves off. People shouted to each other down narrow, tenement streets, or gossiped out of open windows. They reminded me of the interconnections of life in a tropical forest, tree to tree, vine to vine.

Christmas came along, and with it the symbol of Santa Claus. My sister and I discovered very early that it was not Santa Claus who filled the stockings and left the presents under the tree. Nor was it a real Santa Claus we met on the streets. There were dozens of him, standing out in front of the department stores, with their white beards and rumpled red and white suits, shaking their little bells: "Jingle, jingle, and a Ho, Ho, Ho!"

"Hello, Sonny. I know Santa is going to be good to you this year." And he usually was, almost too good to be true. A brightly lit tree stood in the living room, covered with pretty glass balls, with presents for the whole family on the floor beneath it, wrapped in fresh white paper and red ribbon. Every year, we looked forward to it. The next day, I looked out the window, and there was the tree, stripped of its finery, lying out in the grimy backyard, bereft of the star that had been fixed to its leader.

During the Depression, the streets outside were dark and cold. In some parts of the city, there were lines of long-coated men shuffling forward to get their ration of soup. Others sat in front of boxes on street corners, selling apples. On a clear night, the light of all the city's towers almost blotted out the stars, while the bitterly poor, and the drunks, slept in the stairwells.

On a wood road near our house in New Hampshire there was a stand of white pine which later was almost completely knocked down by the hurricane of 1938. It was not unlike a church. The trees must have been at least a century old. There were long aisles between them and vaulted arches high above the ground. The sky showed between them in clear, blue patches like stained glass windows. In the summertime, yellow sunlight flooded through their boughs, which stirred gently over my head. As night came on, the light lowered down their trunks, and they received the darkness as they always had, in a religious silence.

As a boy, in the city or at school, I don't suppose I was particularly conscious of my surroundings in a spiritual sense. I followed order, lessons, and precepts as well as I could. If I spent some time dreaming instead of paying attention, it is possible that I was not yet sure what kind of a world it was that made such demands on me. I also sensed that there was another world of deep and wonderful possibilities waiting for me outside.

In the American Museum of Natural History, where my father worked as an archaeologist, there was an exhibit of timber wolves chasing deer across the snow, with a forest of snow-laden spruce in the background, all covered by the light of the moon. This exhibit was in a side corridor off the main floor. You entered it through curtains that provided a cover of darkness. I felt such enchantment in it that my father could hardly persuade me to come away.

I left my fleeting forest Indians behind me a long time ago, along with my romantic, storybook, childhood world. It was many years, in fact, before I met an original. He was an Alaskan native who I heard reading from an Inuit translation of the Book of Common Prayer. Soon after the end of World War II, I also saw Pueblo Indians in a deer dance. They descended a hillside at dawn, with the graceful gait of a file of deer. I have learned how bitterly dispossessed these first Americans were, impoverished, leading degraded lives and denied their sacred spaces in the land. The fact that many continue to dance is a tribute to religious feelings not easily suppressed, after tens of thousands of years. I am a tourist, an outsider, at these ceremonies. I am part of a world that concentrates more on its right to possess the earth than on cultivating right relationships with it. We ignore the deeper reality that a land is better known through respecting its mysteries than by putting it on a shopping list.

The New Hampshire trees are the same now, even taller than I once knew them, where they have been allowed to grow. I hardly know who I was or what stages I went through to reach the present. The greater world with its massive invasions and disruptions gives few of us any sense of continuity or stability. Millions have been even more dispossessed in this century than were the Native Americans. But an earth dance, with shimmering light, still threads its way between the trees I once grew up with. I am a part, or particle, of it; and I have now learned that there is a sacred alliance between a white pine in New Hampshire and a cottonwood in South Dakota.

The Badlands of South Dakota is a barren plateau made up of ancient marine sediments eroded into fantastic forms. They are as distant from a wooded New England landscape as can be imagined. From spring and on into late summer and fall, it can be scorchingly hot, and only occasional traveling thunderclouds bring any moisture. A few years ago, my friend Gemma Lockhart took me out there to visit a man she much loved and admired named Fools Crow, the ceremonial chief and wise leader of the Sioux. (Gemma's mother was a Lakota Sioux from the Rosebud Reservation, and her father was an Irish railroad engineer, now living near Rapid City.) Fools Crow, then nearing one hundred years of age, lived in a little plain house on the Pine Ridge Reservation, not far from Wounded Knee and its tragic cemetery. It was there, in 1890, that three hundred starving and despairing Sioux, including many women and children, were massacred. Those who survived escaped the white cavalry soldiers by fleeing down deep gullies and ravines that led away from the line of fire. Evidently, some of the soldiers involved were taking revenge for the defeat of the vainglorious General Custer at the battle of the Little Big Horn in 1876. But Wounded Knee could hardly be described as a battle. Unarmed Indians were torn to pieces by Hotchkiss guns, and their bodies dumped into an open trench, where the cemetery is now located.

The massacre had its inception and excuse in the Ghost, or Spirit, Dance, part of a new religion among the Plains

Indians. They had been defeated, exiled from their territories, and confined to reservations, while the buffalo, on which their lives and ceremonies depended, had been slaughtered. Through the practice of the Ghost Dance, the inner life of the people was to be revived, their spiritual destinies assured again. The buffalo would come back and the white man would disappear. All this, to a hard-headed white man, descended from violent pioneers, might have amounted only to a desperate innocence. Yet the dance was performed with intense religious fervor; it spread like wildfire. The Ghost Dance was fundamental to a revival of the spirit world that had always been the foundation of Sioux existence and belief. On the final, terrible day at Wounded Knee, the white agent at the Pine Ridge Reservation seems to have panicked. Thinking that the intensity of the dancing signaled an Indian uprising, he called in the army.

As Gemma Lockhart heard it from an old Sioux woman named Hattie Clifford, now dead, the cavalry had gathered the people in a circle and said that they were going to be given soup to eat. " 'And then,' Hattie said, 'they took that big gun on the hill, and went like this.' She clapped her hands together. They moved wildly with emotion, their fingers spread out, gesturing, stabbing at me, again and again. 'And they killed all the people.' "

When we arrived at the house, Fools Crow was sitting in a low chair. He was a grave old man, with a look of unshakable dignity and faith. He wore a black coat and gray trousers, and had a queue tied at the back of his neck. Since he only spoke in his native tongue, his son Joe served as his interpreter. I was not sure what to ask him, but I did manage to come out with a couple of questions, one of which was about prayer. What was its meaning?

"We pray to the Great Spirit," he answered, "to ask for and to receive his help." (Traditionally, the Sioux believed in a mysterious, creative power called Wakonda that filled the earth and moved the stars.)

Through prayer too, Fools Crow said, one makes things happen. Prayer joins the visible to the invisible world. It makes us communicants in the universe, part of all that lives. I also asked him about *thunder beings*, which I had heard of before in this land of seasons punctuated by thunder and lightning.

"They," he said, "are the spirits of our dead ancestors. They live behind the thunder, and are consulted through prayer."

I thought I was hearing distant echoes in his speech of a very ancient culture, praying, singing, dancing before the Great Mystery.

The plainness of the small room in which the old man sat was a testimony to his character. It was empty of possessions, and of any need to possess. As a wise advisor and healer to his people, Fools Crow had been given many presents, but he gave them all away. (It is the habitual way of the Lakota that if you love or value something highly, you give it away.)

When it was time for Gemma and me to leave, Fools Crow stood up in his serious age and dignity, and gently waved good-bye from the doorway.

Outside Fools Crow's house was a bare-limbed tree, and on it offerings had been hung, gaily colored cloths, like so many flags. It had been the center of a Sun Dance. Fools Crow had brought back this ceremony, teaching it to his people after it had been banned.

"The white people," I was told by Gemma, "knew that

the Sun Dance made us Indians strong. So in the latter part of the nineteenth century, the U.S. government made it illegal. The most sacred ceremony of the Sioux was against the law." In a sense, Fools Crow's restoration of it reopened a part of the American sky to sacred principles.

The Sun Dance tree is a young cottonwood, chosen by the spiritual leader. When it is cut down, the cross section of the trunk reveals the shape of a star. A hole is dug in the center of the ceremonial circle, over which an open arbor will be constructed. Then a pipe, representing the sacred pipe of the Sioux, is placed in the hole, followed by the tree, which symbolizes the great sky, the whole embracing universe, and every living thing.

With each colored cloth on the tree, hung there by the dancers, goes a prayer, one of thanks, or entreaty, perhaps a prayer to the Great Spirit to heal the sick. The cloths are first prepared by putting a pinch of tobacco on them. Then, praying all the while, the dancer folds his cloth in the four directions, west, north, east, and south. It is tied with string, sinew, or thread, and then hung on the tree as a prayer.

The total involvement of the dancers with their songs leads to an annual cleaning and renewal of the spirit. Beyond any material thing, each participant offers his whole self to the Great Spirit without reservation.

"The songs," I am told, "are beautiful. The smell is of sweet smoke and sage. Everything in the arbor circle begins and ends with the sun."

The Sun Dance ceremony may have once been far more elaborate and intensely sacrificial than it is today. It was once part of the ritual for the young men of the Lakota and the Ponca tribes to have skewers inserted through their chests and shoulders. These were tied by long cords to the rafters of a lodge, or to buffalo skulls on the ground, so that the men strained against them as they danced, until they tore themselves loose. Among most other tribes, this self-mortifying practice was either voluntary, or not in use.

The culture that gave rise to the Sun Dance was not only subdued, it was almost completely dispersed and destroyed. And yet in its revived form, the ceremony retains a sacrificial element. The dancers subordinate the self to the mysteries and the great powers of the natural world. We too, no matter how dominating our culture may be, are still the subjects of the unconquerable, life-giving sun. Immortal messages are still waiting for us out of the sky, and through the dark thunder in the hills.

I can only write distantly about the Native Americans. They are new to me. The world of the Lakota is a quiet, private, and secret one. Their most important value is silence. This can help explain why their faith has survived to the extent that it has, in spite of the devastating intrusions of the modern world. Silence as a virtue had its obvious advantage in hunting, or in keeping a baby quiet when an enemy was passing by.

The Lakota language itself is also protective of the inner self, which is why translations into English often fail to convey the real meaning of what is being said.

The American Indian lacked a written language in the first place. They used spoken words to express the depth of their feelings, out of which they prayed, sang, and told their stories with great eloquence. Their words are full of subtleties that most white people are unable to detect.

The old leader was popularly known and referred to as Fools Crow, but, as he once declared to his people: "I am Eagle Bear," which is literally translated as Wombli Mato, but among the Sioux this is reversed, as Mato Wombli. He was seldom called that during his lifetime, but the people knew who he was. The real name among the Sioux is not spoken casually. This is not so much a matter of a closeted reserve, as a respect for personal identity equated with the spirit.

Fools Crow died in peace, in the company of his family, at the age of ninety-nine, in the winter of 1989. The funeral lasted four days and four nights. During this period, he was constantly guarded by a warrior bearing the Eagle Staff of the Sioux, and at night there were two guards, changing every half hour. Day and night, his people came to stand by his coffin and tell stories of Fools Crow. They all worked together on preparations for the funeral, and cooked around the clock to ensure that food was ready at all times.

On the final day, his devoted people filed past his body to say good-bye to their leader, and to shake hands with members of his family before going to wait outside the schoolhouse where he lay. He was to be carried in a buckboard to his grave, as his father had been before him, and to be escorted by eight pallbearers on horseback, wearing war bonnets. There were many other horses present as well, for medicine men, and for other riders at the funeral. The horses were all standing quietly outside, but at the very moment Fools Crow's body was brought out of the building, as Gemma Lockhart told it to me, the horses all started whinnying and screaming. "It was one of the most beautiful things I think I will ever experience," Gemma said. "And maybe it is because of the way I know horses. But I know horses know and they talk. They know what is in the wind."

Gemma told me that they put Fools Crow in the back

of the wagon and started off, traveling west and then south about five and a half miles to the hill where they buried him. With the buckboard all the way went a paint horse with no rider, carrying Fools Crow's war bonnet, and it was followed by a white colt. Some eight hundred to a thousand of his people were present when they buried Fools Crow in the small graveyard plot, and together they sang an honoring or death song for Eagle Bear, Mato Wombli, which had never been sung before and never will be again.

Outside my window there is a rooted, self-renewing evergreen, fifty feet tall, its branches laden with sparkling snow. It is a reminder, like those small nursery trees that at Christmastime are brought into millions of homes, of a vast continent whose great forests are still being ignorantly and recklessly cut down. We place a star on top of the tree and presents at its foot, but if it represents no more than property, it can give us nothing.

At some of the Sun Dance ceremonies, the tree is thanked for having sacrificed its life. In a similar way, a campfire is sometimes thanked for its warmth, energy, and protection. Thank the fire, thank the tree which has a star at its core, for lifting us into the company of the universe.

In Fools Crow's humble vision, all material possessions are given away. The ceremony with the tree at its center honors that blessed poverty. Real riches lie in the commitment of mind and heart to that greater space where every form of life has its distinction.

I am back now to where I was as a boy. It was a time when I wanted to know so much more than I had been told, when I sensed that all the freedom I then desired was outside somewhere, waiting to be found. It was that space where the bear and the buffalo were forever moving on.

I walk out into the cold winter night of New England. The sky is wonderfully clear, and all the great yellow stars are suspended, but at the same time flinging out over infinite reaches. Awesomely distant though they are, they seem to be cascading down, pouring out their light toward the dark ground that lies all around me. The steadfast tree, shaped like a flame, seems to be rising toward them, just as it rises toward the sun. I feel the tension between the forest pinnacles and that vast, blazing depth where everything is born.

Stranded

I had heard about the blackfish, also called pilot whales or potheads, from the time I moved to Cape Cod, but until recently I had never seen a live one. I did once come across some skeletons lined up along a local beach. The whales had apparently been part of a pod composed of family groups, because there were a number of young ones among them. According to local reports, the whales had died on this shore in the 1930s and been uncovered years later by storm waves.

Storms often bring revelations of hidden history in this sandy, malleable land. They periodically bury the evidence and then unearth it again. Not long ago, during a winter walk along the Great Beach, which faces the open Atlantic, I saw what looked like a giant sea turtle ahead of me, a dark brown, rounded back. It turned out to be the half-buried section of a hull from a wrecked sailing vessel, battered but well crafted, with wooden pegs holding the planks together. Since the use of iron instead of wood for larger ships came in during the latter part of the nineteenth century, I supposed that this was a lighter, smaller craft, perhaps a hundred years old. The surviving portion of the boat was about fifteen feet long. Four days later, after a storm that kept the wind booming all night while heavy waves smashed onto the beach, displacing and relocating huge volumes of sand, the wreck had completely disappeared, tossed back into the nineteenth century.

A few miles from where I saw this remnant, archaeologists were excavating an Indian site at the head of the beach, working intensively against the possibility that another storm might wash away all their work. In the eroding banks of peat above the shore, they had uncovered large trees that might be several thousand years old. On the evidence of an archaic spear point, they think that ten thousand years ago the bank was in a sheltered area five miles behind the present shoreline. So the world ocean beyond carves the land away and spreads its waters over whole continents, with supreme disregard of the way we measure time and history.

Under its shifting sands, the Great Beach hides the wrecks of a hundred ships or more, the debris of civilization. Where the beach slopes off into the Atlantic in fog, driving rain, sleet, sunlight, and showers, it becomes a broad highway of transformations, of tricks and illusions. Mysterious creations seem to rise before your eyes and disappear. The green, primordial surf pounds down the shore, carrying intermittent sounds of dying ships, falling houses, and crashing rocks along with the clatter of its stones. Then it subsides, to repeat its histories. Nothing can claim it but creation.

The blackfish are relatively small—only twenty feet long—as compared to the big whales like finbacks and humpbacks, which are up to sixty or sixty-five feet in length. But they weigh some eighteen hundred pounds, two hun-

dred pounds short of a ton. They once provided an extra
source of income for generations of shore fishermen living
in the towns along the inner circle of Cape Cod Bay. The
whales were valued not for their meat but for their head oil,
which was refined and used to lubricate light machinery,
clocks, and watches. It fetched sixty-five dollars a gallon,
good money in those days. The oil came from a lump the
size of a watermelon in the whales' heads, which gave the
animals the name of potheads. In the 1850s, according to
Henry Kittredge's book *Cape Cod*, Captain Daniel Rich cut
his mark on the sides of seventy-five blackfish stranded on
the beach between Wellfleet and Truro and made one thousand dollars out of them.

When the spouts or rounded backs of the blackfish appeared offshore, townspeople would rush down to the shore
and launch their dories or other small boats. They would
surround the whales, yelling and beating on the water with
their oars. The quarry panicked, headed in, and beached
themselves. The "shore whalers," as they were called, then
got to work with knives and lances, killing the poor beasts
with great vigor. They usually shared the profits on an equal
basis, possibly because there were not many lawyers and
insurance people around in those days to complicate the
business.

This method of whaling was convenient for those who
did not want to hunt whales over deep water, and the whales
aroused great excitement in the towns where they landed.
"Drift whales" were thought to be a blessing sent through
the grace of God, and in one instance grateful parishioners
of the church in Eastham used part of the whaling proceeds
to pay the minister's salary.

Those of us who rarely see blackfish and who certainly

have never seen half a town engaged in cutting them up would not enjoy watching the process. Phil Schwind, a native of the Cape who died in the spring of 1992 at the age of eighty-five, has described a scene from the 1940s in his book *Cape Cod Fisherman*:

> Then the murder started. I know of no other word that would fit. Those great beasts, their thin, external skin as black and shiny as patent leather, beat the sand with their tails; they sighed and cried like monstrous babies. Their gasping was pathetic to hear as the tide ran out and left them helplessly high and dry, but what fisherman stops to listen when there is money to be made? Armed with a razor-sharp lance on the end of a ten-foot hickory pole, Cal came up behind the flipper of the nearest blackfish and beat the creature three or four times over the head. When I protested, Cal explained, "You have to warn them you're here. I've lanced fish I didn't warn first and had them jump clear off the sand. Somebody could get hurt that way."
>
> Cal drove the lance into the side of the creature, again and again, trying to make a bigger and bigger hole. Blood poured out in torrents, "gushed" is a more exact word. It splattered us and dyed the beach a bright red. One and then another he killed, working down the beach through the whole school.
>
> It was dark before we finished lancing; my job was to hold a flashlight so Cal could see. Sometimes the fish were so close together we had to climb on one while it was still alive to lance another. Behind us blackfish in their death throes were heaving and moaning with blood-choked sighs. Their great tails lashed the sand, making a sound like a whole herd of horses galloping across hard ground.

Little more of the blackfish was used than the forty- to fifty-pound chunks in their heads, although their thick coats of blubber contained tons of oil, and their bodies contained tons of good meat. After the cutting was over, the remains were buried in the sand above the tideline before the stench became unbearable. Waste has been an almost built-in part of the economic thinking in this country.

Edward Howe Forbush, in his *Birds of Massachusetts*, published in 1920, describes a trip he took in 1876 to the St. John River region of the Florida wilderness, where there were multitudes of shorebirds along the coasts and lagoons. Arriving at Lake George, he saw "vast dense flocks" of wild ducks, a mile or more in length. Eagles, hawks, and owls were common, as were wild turkeys. This original abundance was irresistible:

> Practically all tourists were armed with rifles, shotguns, revolvers, or all three. These armed men lined the rails of the steamboats and shot ad libitum at alligators, waterfowl or anything that made an attractive target. There were practically no restrictions on shooting, although the steamers never stopped to gather in the game, but left it to lie where it fell.

Frank Dobie, who wrote extensively about the traditions, animals, and folklore of Texas, said that the treatment of wildlife by the pioneers was "beyond belief." Even after the fates of the passenger pigeon and the buffalo were well known, people considered everything wild that came before their eyes fair game.

In his book *Karankaway Country*, Frank Dobie's friend Roy Bedichek, the Texas naturalist, describes an annual event of the late nineteenth century, in which so-called sportsmen would gather together as if on a fairground to shoot all the prairie chickens within range. These birds were males during their spring courtship rituals. First prize went to the gunner who shot the most birds, judged by the height of his pile of corpses. After the festivities were over all the piles were left to rot on the ground.

The relentless gambling with the resources of a continent continued until conservation laws were enacted, but our wasteful habits have continued. The early killing has left a residue of indifference to animals that is shared to a large extent by millions of Americans.

The blackfish, more often called pilot whales these days so as not to confuse them with fish, a race to which they do not belong, feed on squid in deep water along the edge of the continental shelf. During the summer and early autumn, the squid move closer inshore to feed, and the whales follow them. It was estimated that in the waters off Newfoundland during the late 1950s some forty-seven thousand pilot whales were taken. The original population is thought to have been no more than sixty thousand.

The tendency of these animals to herd closely together in family groups made it easier to drive them inshore. But what makes them strand voluntarily, if that is the right way to describe it? Theories have been advanced about parasitic infections of the inner ear, or inattention to what kind of bottom the whales might find themselves in, especially during frenzied feeding. It is possible that the whales become confused during migration when they swim out of deep water into Cape Cod Bay. The Cape is like a hook, starting from its stem on the mainland and curving around to its northern tip at Provincetown. The waters of the bay are relatively shallow, no more than eighty feet in depth. A sandy reef or bar near the mouth might confuse the whales if they swam inside it, and could not find their way out, or a storm might come up to further disturb their sense of direction. They might then swim in toward gradually shallowing waters and become even more disoriented as their geomagnetic sense was scrambled. It is also theorized that beaches with flat profiles disturb the whales' ability to echolocate. Whatever the explanation, after countless generations the pilots seem to have been unable to hand down the knowledge that a trap like Cape Cod must be avoided.

Each school has at least one leader, and if the leader panics, giving calls of distress, the rest follow. Phil Schwind, who is of the opinion that the leader is not necessarily a male, says these animals could be herded like sheep. People used to drive around them with their boats, which by the 1940s were equipped with motors. Their method was to wait until the moment when the tide started to turn back and then cut off one of the animals, which might be of either sex, and wait for the rest to follow. (After the forties, the once-precious head oil was superseded in the marketplace by refined petroleum and no longer had any value.)

The blackfish will not be separated, even under extreme conditions. They have a powerful sense of unity, and they are highly sensitive to each other's movements, needs, and inclinations. Such highly social animals communicate through a complex repertoire of underwater calls. Apparently each individual has a distinctive whistle. Pilot whales belong to the family of dolphins, so you might suppose them to have similar ways of communicating, although their social structure is much more tightly knit and familial than that of other species in the group. Dolphins trade information through a variety of clicks, whistles, and other strange sounds. A group of dolphins makes decisions as to when to move out to sea from near the coast, or when to go fishing at night. According to Kenneth Norris in his book *Dolphin Days*, about the spinner dolphins of the Pacific:

> Each school member can detect the emotional level and alertness of the others, just as the wolf can tell by the itch and tension in another's call where it is in the chase. Under the greatest excitement, tension on its vocal chords may cause its voice to break just as our own voices break in heightened circumstances.

Norris supposes an

> emotional glue that gives richness and nuance to a metaphoric communication system. Just as our spirits rise when we are listening to a symphony and its tempo increases, . . . so might something like emotion be transmitted throughout a school. . . . We routinely talk about future events when we say something simple like, "Let's go to the store." But the dolphin school, it seems, must match event and action while it acts out an emotionally based metaphor of what is going on.

What their refined use of signals means at any given moment remains to be understood and can only be found out, if at all, through patient, untiring research and a painstaking accumulation of data. Dr. Norris indicates that isolated signals may be symbolic, a given sound indicating a given circumstance. That, he says, is about halfway to being a word.

In a society so estranged from animals as ours, we often fail to credit them with any form of language. If we do, it comes under the heading of communication rather than speech. And yet the great silence we have imposed on the rest of life contains innumerable forms of expression. Where does our own language come from but this unfathomed store that characterizes innumerable species?

We are now more than halfway removed from what the unwritten word meant to our ancestors, who believed in the original, primal word behind all manifestations of the spirit. You sang because you were answered. The answers came from life around you. Prayers, chants, and songs were also responses to the elements, to the wind, the sun and stars, the Great Mystery behind them. Life on earth springs from a collateral magic that we rarely consult. We avoid the unknown as if we were afraid that contact would lower our sense of self-esteem.

*N*ow I come to my first meeting with live pilot whales. It was on September 30, 1991. I had driven down to the parking lot at the head of the local beach in East Dennis where I often walk, especially at low tide, but I was stopped by a policeman. He told me that seventeen whales were stranded on the beach. So I left the car farther back in town and walked to the beach the long way around, through the thickets and dunes behind it. When I reached the beach, I saw a line of onlookers who were cordoned off on the sands just above the waterline. In their midst was a small, young whale lying dead on the sand. Others, still alive, had been removed and taken to the nearby channel of Sesuit Harbor to recuperate. In the shallow inshore waters were five knots of rescuers, or would-be rescuers, each holding on with quiet but obviously weary determination to a large, shiny black whale. The backs of the pilot whales were exposed, and the rescuers kept pouring water over them to keep them from drying out. In one case, a huge eighteen-hundred-pound animal was being carried onto the beach on a front-end loader by a number of people who had managed to get a stretcher under it. A line of people in deeper water farther out was trying to prevent another whale from moving in. The silent insistence in the animals was stunning to watch.

The rescuers were showing the strain. "I'm tired," one woman was heard to say. "It's more frustrating than discouraging. You try to help these animals but you don't know what to do. I wish we could learn the language of pilot whales."

In a later conversation, Phil Schwind, with memories of older and rougher realities, said to me that he felt sorry for those poor volunteers standing in cold water up to their waists for hours on end, desperately trying to hold back the whales, as if they could stop nature.

What nature is, we seldom seem to know. It is hard for us as "thinking animals" to understand behavior like that of the stranding whales, and we are too ready to confuse it with mass psychology. Yet in the great seas where these animals live, cohesion is a strategy for survival. When something happens to one animal, all the rest are in danger and respond.

The whales at East Dennis had been part of a larger group that had stranded four days before in Truro, farther down the shore of the Cape, where an effort had been made to save them from themselves. Later on, some of the survivors of the East Dennis stranding moved to Yarmouth. It was highly discouraging to the rescue teams, who had congratulated themselves on managing to persuade a whale to

stay off the beach and swim away, to have it strand somewhere else. Other whales would simply wait offshore until
the tide lowered and then strand themselves again.

During this period of stranding, five young whales, first
three and then two more, were thought to be in good
enough condition to be moved to the New England Aquarium. After a period of rest and careful feeding, they were
successfully released at sea and their movements tracked in
the months that followed. Science benefits from these efforts. The whales are an important source of information,
a good, long-term investment in knowledge. Methods improve. Institutions are encouraged to tackle larger species
of whales in the future, to add even more knowledge and
hope. These very laudable efforts are also part of our need
as a society to impose our will and to succeed in solving
problems that face us. This need brings strong emotions
with it — tears for hope, and tears for failure. But in the final
analysis, we do not know why pilot whales strand, or what
we could possibly do to prevent it.

There was something about that scene on the beach, with
its ardent, tired people and the silent black whales bent on
moving in to the terrible shore that affected me profoundly.
As I was starting to leave, a buried memory welled up inside
me, a waking dream. I remembered a feeling of being alone,
of being detached, pulled away from all familiar surroundings and support. It had come to me a long time ago, when
I was a boy, and I vaguely associated it with the dark weight
of the city where we lived. Perhaps it was the immense
drawing power of the ocean at my feet that helped bring
this dreamlike memory out into the open. It was a very real

feeling of removal and dislocation, but I do not equate it with fear, or dread anticipation of what was to come next. I had simply been pulled away from all familiarity and faced with some inexorable darkness of cavernous dimensions. But in some way, the memory brought me closer to those deep-sea animals than I could have imagined possible.

As I walked away down the beach, I passed a flock of sandpipers standing and scuttling along the wet sands at the edge of the beach. A blue light was cast around them from the water and the sky. Beyond them the ever present gulls watched the horizon, and a few crows scavenged for food over the tidelands. The sanderlings flew up spontaneously and sped off to land farther down the shore.

Ringing the coasts of the world, the birds are one measure of its tidal complexities. Each kind seems to stand out as an embodiment of light, commanded by the unknown depths of creation. They are on earth's inspired and urgent business, carrying its many worlds of being far into a future that requires of each of them a certain perfection.

Birds, fish, whales, and human beings live on the edge of oblivion, which often snatches them out of the air or the depths of the sea. During their varying spans of life they are all creation's people, each singularly endowed to follow out the life of the planet. Without this great company we would hang in a void. A chance meeting with a dying whale, a flock of sanderlings, or a passing bird testing the atmosphere may be a revelation, however fleeting, of the underlying powers that lead us on and define our being. We come closest to nature, in its beginnings and endings, its Alphas and Omegas, in the darkest corners of our dreams.

On a recent visit to the city, I learned that pilot whales are known to dive down to at least eighteen hundred feet below the surface of the ocean. I was repeating this to my wife as we were traveling downtown in a bus. I heard a schoolboy sitting opposite us ask, "Do they really dive that deep?" When I answered, "I believe so," he turned his head and lapsed into a reverie, where we left him as we climbed down from the bus.

Listening to
the Wind

$\mathcal{I}$ was surrounded by cultivation, order, and control as I was growing up, and when, in later years, I was confronted by chaotic circumstances, I was grateful for such training. Original, native space, on the other hand, was never cultivated. I learned to count on everything that came from it, unannounced. I remember a wonderful spring day in the city when a warm golden light suddenly flooding our street inspired us to open all the doors and windows to the great air. That dark city, with its way of swallowing people whole, had not been able to separate us from the light.

In New Hampshire, the north country, although I had relatively little education in the particulars of nature, I was always conscious of the dark green hills rolling on toward some unseen grandeur in the west.

The waters of the lake were always gently lapping on the rocky shore. The brook that supplied the water for our house ran out of its source on Sunset Hill and down to the lake through the trees. At intervals, the sky would turn a deep slate gray, and a thunderstorm would crash in all around us. Lightning occasionally cracked a tree, and once hit the corner of the house. The lake waters scudded and raced ahead under the concentrated passion of the storm. Bird song, a magic of the elect, lifted out of the trees. Some fifty yards up from the lakeshore was a spring of pure, cold water lying under leaf litter, which I periodically cleared away to drink what my father said was the best water in the state.

I had such accomplices in the electric process of growth, emerging out of dark grounds I was barely conscious of. They led me toward a beginner's "faith in things unseen." Universal life is what we are given, before we start to dissect it.

I followed the facts as they were fed to me, but was also a friend of the intangible. "Is it real?" asks the child, seeing the mounted specimen of a bird. It might be alive, but it does not move. That area between the animate and the in-animate is not easily dismissed by children even with adult suggestions not to touch it, not to swim in it, not to explore it without supervision.

Since everything is unfinished, the young accept the in-tangible as having a life of its own. The sun climbed the steps of the sky in and out of sight. The trees, whose names I had hardly begun to know, were clearly full of undiscov-ered secrets, and the birds appeared in springtime out of nowhere, or everywhere. "All nonsense," said the adults when I blurted out some fanciful notion which did not square with *their* reality. On the surface, I began to give up dreaming, but dreams are subterranean, not controlled.

The world I moved into out of my youth could hardly be described as "practical" and it was far from secure. All the realists were out fighting fires of unreal proportions which they had created. Impermanence led us, and all our vain imaginings. And no fish or flower was given credit for having any experience of its own. The countryside was no longer the safe haven it once had been, and now, where money is valued above life itself, society cannot discriminate between what is useful to it and what is not. Still, we have no other recourse but to follow the wind that leaves us behind but goes on its everlasting business of reconciling and begetting, carrying the signs of an enduring architecture around the globe.

On the sandy peninsula of Cape Cod, as well as the rocky shores of Maine, where we have lived for many years, the wind comes in from all directions, to blow out over the Atlantic. Storm systems, especially between late fall and spring, are the products of vast influence, stretching from the Gulf of Mexico to Labrador, from the Pacific to the Atlantic. The winds join storm tides in carving away the cliffs and headlands of the Cape, and they are constantly reshaping its beaches. In terms of geologic time, this is a fast and relentless process. In another ten thousand years or so, this sandy and vulnerable land will be reduced to some outlying sandy shoals.

This is an ephemeral land, and our occupation of it seems more impermanent every year. The local evidence of a rooted life has largely disappeared. The native speech is seldom heard; the farms and truck gardens are long gone; the old barns converted into housing, or antique stores. Because of a disastrous decline in fish populations, the native fishermen are seldom seen. New developments have been scattered over once "worthless woodlots," and houses are dropped down on bulldozed land as if they had been pre-assembled in the sky. The old sandy, rutted roads have been paved over. The "rural seaside atmosphere" much loved by the Chamber of Commerce can hardly be appealed to any more. All this means that we are now part of mainland America, a nation of itinerants.

Hundreds of thousands of visitors crowd in to shop and lie on the beaches during the summer months. Even the winter traffic has increased with quicker access to town, and a much greater population of the retired. People on wheels are perpetually elevated above the land, speeding everywhere and nowhere, reflecting the restless and distracted character of the world at large. Notwithstanding this abstracted relationship with the land, the tides keep moving in and drawing back in their complex regularity, and the ocean keeps releasing and withholding its passion. This is where we are placed, in spite of ourselves.

In mid-April, three weeks after the vernal equinox, when the seabirds are moving off to their nesting grounds, the clouds on a cool and windy day seem to take the shapes and forms of the tidal world below them. In one part of the sky, smoky clouds spread like a great fan, and in another there are widening patterns of skeletal fish, or fronds of seaweed. A long, wavy line of brant geese flies over the water, forward into the wind. This is a small, compact, handsome bird, once numerous and much prized for its meat. It is now relatively scarce, having suffered a serious decline during the 1930s when a blight nearly wiped out the eel grass the brant depend on for food.

During the months of autumn, the brant are late migrants, flying south from their nesting grounds in the Arctic circle. They winter along the shores of the Carolinas, and on Cape Cod, where their numbers vary from year to year. Flocks of brant heading down from Hudson Bay to New

York are sometimes forced into a more easterly heading by strong, seasonal winds from the northwest and land along the marshes of the inner arm of the Cape. I look forward on any year to seeing these distinguished visitors as they move from one part of the shore to another. Their call is a very distinctive, high-reaching "r-r-r-r- ook" or "cr-r-r-up." One day, when I was walking far out over the sandy flats at low tide, a group of them flew overhead close enough so that I could see their breasts through my field glasses, and I sensed the clean weight of their bodies as they raced through the air, and the fast pulsing of their hearts.

The tidal areas, stretching off at low tide for miles along the horizon, comprise a vast range of seed time and harvest engendered by the shallow seas. I go to them for their wealth, in the midst of a semi-impoverished land, and for visions of new lands and continents far beyond them. When the tide recedes, the flats are like a great plaza, a floor of ripples, ribs, and chains, and show as well the tracks of birds, leading in, over, and away. You can follow the evidence of innumerable holes or burrows, made by various kinds of worms, shrimp, and countless other tidal organisms that range in size from a great sea clam off at the farthest reach of the tide to a tiny purple-hued Gemma clam. This shore life is full of complex associations in a harsh and demanding environment that is changing every day from one form of exposure to another. These plants and creatures live and thrive on the fine edge of flooding and drying out. Each marine community has its own manner of dealing with a world of transformation, a world which never erases their distinctive forms and devices for survival.

The seaweed, more common on the rocky ranges of the coast, are born of and supported by the dynamic motion of the waves. Their slick, leathery skins, their fronds and plumes, and the air bladders that give them buoyancy belong to the oscillation of a wave. They are dragged back by its turbulence from their rocky foothold, carried under the water, and as the waters move forward again, they bob up like corks. The forms of seaweed were built of millions of years of turbulence and forbearance.

These closing and opening communities along the shore do not behave automatically in the face of all the pressures that best them. Their lives are part of an interchange, on a cosmic scale, of moving energies. We may be deluded into thinking that we are on the outside looking in, taking full advantage of our sight and mind, masters of all we enumerate, but all lands and landscapes are creations of what we are unable to conquer on our own.

Sometimes, during late fall and winter into early spring, you can smell a storm coming in on the wind, and sense its pressure in your lungs. Down by the sandy shores, the sand grains are driven into your face, and the wind may almost topple you. Inland, the leafless oaks lean away from the invasion of the salt sea and the air, rocking and swaying. The heavily laden pitch pines are visibly straining from their roots. During strong gusts they look as if they were being forcibly plucked out of the ground. Branches crack, trees fall and, in some areas, litter the landscape. The wind's roar dies down, the seas subside, and the transient land is reduced once more.

The winds that influence birds on their migration, often taking them off course, are also one of their consistent guides, as are the position of the sun over the horizon, the landmarks below them, and an ancient, magnetic pull of direction. The wind joins a reproductive dance across the continent, carrying pollen, seeds, and insects, as well as dust particles for great distances. As the form of seaweed is a rhythmic counterpart of a wave, so land plants are responsive in varying degrees to the wind and the atmosphere. A bit of knowledge that passed me by for many years was that grasses are pollinated by the wind, and that their characteristics reflect it. They are slender, and the stigma of their inconspicuous flowers are feathery so as to catch the pollen grains, which are tiny, light, and dry, easily carried by the air. The grass seeds are also light and small. Flowers designed to attract insects are far more elaborate.

The wind is not specific, but sends the seed ahead indiscriminately, and where it lands it can be tumbled, or washed around, as well as blown, across the varying contours and surfaces of the land. Over the grasslands of the west, the seed is also transported by animals. The hooves of the bison as well as their thick, wooly coats carried seeds, and so did the antelope, prairie dog, coyote, rabbits, and the innumerable mice and voles.

Grass seeds that survive their travels remain dormant for varying lengths of time, while forest seeds germinate quickly, given the right conditions. During periodic years when species of oak drop their acorns like hailstones on the ground, assuring the gray squirrel and the ruffed grouse a good food supply, each acorn wastes no time in thrusting its white root into the soil, so as to give the great structure of an oak tree a sure beginning in its tenure on the land. Where the trees are all cut down for man's temporary convenience, we lose a tenure in our minds.

Adherence, in an age which casts so many time-honored worlds adrift, is to join the wind as it travels over the light

of the waves, and it is to see the wind in the seed, to know
the dedication of the birds on their planetary missions. We
can find neither home nor direction without participation.

In the fall, as a child in New Hampshire, I had a feeling
of "going away," which was not so much a sadness at the
end of summer, and at having to go back to school, but an
inner mood that corresponded with the sailing of the year.
The fire in the trees made me long to go on voyages. There
were leaf spinners all around us in the hazy, blue air. They
were coming down on an invisible decision of the trees to
let them go. They were not dying. They were part of a magical process that denied finality, joining a future regen-
eration of the ground. Out in the wind and the golden
sunlight, they rocked and eddied down, at times skidding
like a bird, then slowly skated in, to be with earth, fire,
water, and air.

To listen to the wind, to join the drifting dance of the
autumn leaves, is to take part in the unity of space. If the
whole world as we use it is ungovernable, then look to the
greater government of the ocean-sea that covers three-
quarters of the planet. If we can only think of ourselves as
a unique species set apart from all others, then we deny the
greater community of the sun, which attends all rituals.

The Grass Dance of the Plains Indians originated among
the Omaha. Central to the ceremony, which included a feast
of dog meat, was a great drum, made out of a cottonwood
tree, and associated with thunder. The drum was used by
the Omaha preparatory to going to war. The transition to
the contemporary form of the dance, as it has been diffused

and changed, is hard to trace. The songs and social features of the Grass Dance as they have been adopted might very well reflect a spiritual need to come out in the open again after dark and terrible times, to join the lasting color and motion of an open world.

The Lakota word for the dance is *wacipi peji*. *Wacipi* means dance, or celebration, and *peji* means grass. Grass is a symbol of *generosity*, a word that seems to have a deeper meaning than the idea of abundance.

In the area where the dance is to take place, a circle of grass is beaten down and flattened, symbolizing the four corners of the world. The life of plants is celebrated in the dance. The Plains tribes use sweet grass, and they make braids out of red grass, which is that same Little Bluestem that grows on my sandy acres. They may also wear long ribbons, reaching down their backs.

"A good grass dancer," I am told, "is so much a part, and moves in the same natural way as the grass itself when winds blow gently through the fields. A grass dancer has a way of moving so that it makes you want to watch him. He is beautiful and he is free."

The dance comes to the people through an ancient, tribal heritage of attention to the earth, and through listening. The plants have spoken to the people through their dreams and visions, and they listen to the wind as the voice of creation. Out in the country of the Great Plains where the wind passes over the dances of the grass elders listened intently to the wind, and though many of them are gone, some remain. These listeners are not common, but if they listen in the right way, they will be spoken to and guided in the right direction. Behind the visible world, the wind carries the word to an attentive listener, out of earth's creation.

"And all your relatives are behind you every step of the way. Your relatives and the Great Spirit."

Our modern, owned world is going deaf from listening to its own answers. Listening to the wind is an exercise in the location and inner sense of a continent we have been leaving behind us in our haste.

Desertion of the Fishes

I knew only a few kinds of fish when I was a boy. On visits to my maternal grandparents in Ipswich, Massachusetts, we went out to sea to catch mackerel in a fishing boat owned by Captain Peabody. Those torpedo-shaped, shiny fish were the sea, for all I knew, its body and its flesh. The lake fish of New Hampshire were more familiar to me, although it took some time, aside from sunfish and bass, to learn the difference between them. I once went running up to the house and declared that I had caught a rare Sunapee trout, and was distressed to learn that it was only a sucker. The big mouth, or black bass, was the one I became most conscious of. When I lay on my stomach and peered down from the dock that jutted out into the lake, I could see bass as they moved slowly and serenely over the rocks on the bottom. We used to fish for them with hooks baited with worms or hellgrammites, wicked looking creatures with pincers on their heads, which I later learned are the larvae of the dobsonfly. I think what most impressed me about that fish, even as it was snatched from its natal depths into the destroying air, was its unhindered distinction. It had a black back and greenish-black sides, like the dark trees that lined the shore. Its fins were very sharp, and it had a reputation for voracity. The fish's white flesh with its delicate black traceries was delicious to eat. I fished on into my teens for black bass from a canoe, a rowboat, and from a fourteen-foot houseboat I built for myself. I explored that lake, in and out, and the bass were with me. I thought of them during the wintertime, when the lake was sealed in by ice, lying semi-dormant, or slowly moving out into deeper water. They were lake keepers, out of its ancient geologic past. I began to see them as being of the essence of all the waters, in somnolence or passion. And one evening many years later, when I passed by those same shores in a sightseeing boat, I thought, a little sadly, of all the magic I had experienced on my own, slowly cruising along in the twilight, with my boat's half-lights on the water. The humanized world had pulled me out of the water and left me gasping on the bank.

Years later, I met another tribe of the great race of fishes, as it swam into freshwater out of the sea during the springtime. When they filled the local brook with their packed, silvery bodies, the alewives, or freshwater herring, were messengers for me of the ocean depths. Now, as they are not much used for food, they cannot be said to deserve the name of neighbors. On their annual migration, as they swim unswervingly upstream against the current to lay their eggs in the headwaters, they have become a spectator sport. The sightseers climb out of the cars to view the alewives; there is an almost violent urgency in those sea animals which is hard to ignore. But as they look into the water, I suspect they no longer see themselves, no longer recognize themselves as fellow inhabitants of an unseen depth.

The other day I stopped by a herring run off the Cape

Cod Canal; it is now walled in with concrete and takes the fish under the highway to their spawning areas on a hillside. The canal is open at another end to saltwater, and the migrating fish can be watched directly as they meet the mouth of the freshwater stream where it pours into the canal. There they circle and coil in the current, hesitate, fall back, and wait, testing a new rhythmic experience, finally to head in and join the ranks filing upstream. I looked down on them from a high bank, instead of at ground level, of the homestream and valley where I had followed them before. I began to see them for the first time in terms of their individual movements with respect to each other. The alewives slowly drifted along, always heading up, but occasionally changing position and dropping back. It is not an entirely anonymous crowd in the sense that with their big open-lidded staring eyes, and their highly sensitive skins, the fish are aware not only of their fellow migrants, but of their position in the stream and of its opposing banks. I could see individuals adjusting to one another, with a slight turning of the head. It is acceptable to think of schooling fish as regimented, acting like reflex mechanisms, unable to think. But they are sent ahead, in their great reproductive drive, by the power of the waters that endows all creatures with the varying facets of its genius. I see those fish as my progenitors.

I climbed into my car and drove back home again, in heavy springtime traffic. Each of us, encased in our own machines, had very little awareness of the others, eyes straight ahead, hands on the wheel, as we headed off to separate destinations. Seen from a helicopter, automotive traffic may be resolved into regular, fluid patterns, but it is made up of people who never met each other before. Each of us is centered on the road ahead, eyes forward, not unlike the fish, but we are always half-conscious, in our separate ways, that what has been set going might get out of control.

We move out on our dry highways as if we were permanently elevated above the land. The more acceleration is engineered into our automobiles, the more disconnected we become.

Fish are an image of the once pure waterways of the continent. They have followed the veins and arteries of the earth over an irretrievable past. When fish disappear, as they are now doing at a terrible rate, it is as if we were losing our communion with a priceless heritage. And yet the age-old alliance between people and fish is almost lost to a world of giant supermarkets, with products that come from anywhere and nowhere. Indifference is helping to kill off the once-sacred cod. What we are no longer dependent on is not in our vision of reality.

I remember, when staying at my Ipswich grandparents' house, that hardly a day passed by when we were not made aware of how close the fish were in our lives. Children were fed cod liver oil for its vitamins (it was also a cure for rickets). It went with some difficulty down my throat. We ate codfish cakes, boiled cod with egg sauce, flounder, halibut, and haddock, as well as mackerel for which we went out fishing with hand lines. Fish were said to be inexhaustible, like the sea itself, and we were brought up with the parable of the loaves and the fishes. To experience the local waters in terms of fish was to know the everlasting waves, and to smell the wind that brings the taste of salt miles inland from the coast. My grandfather was descended from British immigrants to the New World who settled in Ipswich and started a farm in 1638. He was, so far as I could tell, a contented man, secure in the feeling that his descendants would own and manage the land and the farm for the indefinite future. Inscribed in tiles over the family fireplace was this verse from Alexander Pope's "Ode on Solitude":

> Happy the man whose wish and care
>   A few paternal acres bound,
> Content to breathe his native air
>   In his own ground.

My grandfather's ambition never seemed to soar much farther than the family farm. The house was built well before World War I, one of the great disruptions in human history. It burned down after his death, though the farm still exists, and is well managed during a period when so many of them have been forced out of existence. I doubt that he was ever fully aware of the growing impermanence in American life.

Some years ago, I was sent by a travel magazine to write an article about Greenland. A fairly small number of us traveled by boat, a renovated ferry, up the west coast as far as Disko Bay, stopping off at villages along the way. On our return, we spent a couple of days in the capital city of Godthåb. There I walked to the marketplace where they sold fish. The great bodies of cod, halibut, and others, slick, shining white bellies and variegated speckled gray bodies, were lying out on open tables. It was a revelation of stature, an almost primal abundance, although it was said that there were fish enough off Greenland for a once small population of eight thousand, but not for a growing one which had

reached forty thousand. The city gave evidence of the dis-
possession of the native fishing and hunting people who had
once lived in isolated places along the coast. Many had now
been forced to live in gray concrete apartments, which they
must have had a hard time recognizing as home. Living
there meant the abandonment of the mighty sky and loss
of the weather from which they had always taken their
bearings.

In Greenland, the largest island in the world, I had never
felt so close to elemental scale, the great beauty of the unconquerable. Traveling between towering icebergs, in sight
of snowy mountains and on the edge of the ice cap, thirty
meters thick at its center, that covers most of Greenland, I
looked out over the dark sea and thought: "I could never
survive in this land. I would soon be lost, or freeze to death."
But the terms that magnificent land laid down transcended
anything so temporary.

I was not prepared for the sheer glory of the Arctic in
its open reception of the light, nor for the sense of unfath-
omable age, seen in bare, worn rock, which seemed to date
back almost as far as the origins of the earth itself. Some
newcomers to these lands have felt highly vulnerable; others,
perhaps for the same reason, look away, bored by the sce-
nery. But for many it is exhilarating to be in a land of such
uncompromising purity. The dark and shining spaces give
each form of life a stature of its own. Caribou, arctic foxes,
gulls, seals and seabirds, the ravens I heard conversing in
their ancient tongue, and the huge fish I saw in the marketplace, all stood out in relief, inheritors of a majestic past.

Life for the Inuit seal hunters and fishermen in this uncompromising world was one of great hardship. For modern
people determined to keep elemental exposure at a safe dis-

tance, it would be unendurable. Knud Rasmussen, the great explorer and anthropologist, born in Greenland, knew those people. He said of them that they had "a humility in the face of the pressures of life for which we must surely envy them."

"They had a harsh, natural life, but such an abundance of soul among them that the singing and the competition of poetry had become an absolute necessity."

"The joy these people had in the power, the warmth of words never ceased to impress me."

Our world has been inclined to call such ancient cultures "primitive." The Netsilik Eskimo seal hunter developed a precise technology of hunting tools made of local materials such as bone and sinew from the seals they hunted. Cro Magnon men, thirty thousand years ago, showed a visionary artistry in their cave paintings which has not been surpassed since. What is to be said of a society which uses its advanced technology to damage or destroy the earth beyond its capacity to sustain us? Are we not primitive, to a tragic degree?

On a trip to Newfoundland, some thirty years ago, I stood on top of a high cliff overlooking the sea and watched two fishermen in a deep Newfoundland dory pulling in a wealth of fish such as I had never seen before. One great wet and shining cod after another was hauled into their boat until it was almost fully loaded with them. One of the men saw me and waved, a triumphant smile on his face.

On one rocky shore, I also watched the capelin "roll" in. Capelin are a major food of the cod and other fish, as well as of whales and seabirds. The dark waters just offshore were packed with their green bodies. They looked like beds of eel grass, with its long stems streaming in the tidal current. The capelin, small, slim-bodied fish somewhat resembling the smelt, "roll" in to a beach at the peak of extreme high tide, quickly laying a prodigious number of eggs, which are sticky and adhere to the stone and gravel surface of the shore. The capelin range widely over the high seas of the North Atlantic, but are seldom seen in great abundance close to land except during the spawning season.

All along the shore where these multitudes, one of the principal foods of the ocean, were massing, hundreds of black-legged kittiwakes had gathered, white as snow and wildly, excitedly crying. They circled, dipped down to the surface, and raced back and forth. This was high drama, an annual marine event that called many different forms of life together, to share in the abiding fertility of the seas.

Where are they now, the capelin and the cod? The only place most of us are likely to see a large specimen of an adult codfish is in an aquarium, where it survives as a remnant of a disappearing world.

At the aquarium, I am an urban dweller, an onlooker, and a curiosity seeker. It is superior entertainment to climb the stairs while looking in at the fish on various levels of the great circular tank. The famous cod is there, once the mainstay of offshore fishing, along with the haddock. With its freckled skin, broad fins, and a barbel under its chin, it moves at a lordly pace, around and around. The quick dancers and the slow pacers are there, along with those that hide and skulk in caves and crevices. The vegetarians, scavengers, and predators appear and reappear on their various levels. Shimmer schools flash by, and the close ranks of hunting packs that follow their food in the open seas. They swim before our eyes as major players in the wide theatre of the world. Some were born of the thunderous gray and white Atlantic, others in the warm, transparent waters of the Caribbean, reflecting the brilliant color spectrum of the sun. Out of the ocean's primal history, they take part in the revolutions of light. Clad in silver and gold, they could never be confused with the castaways, the homeless, and the impoverished.

And so, I walk out and back into the cavernous city, where I can hide or join the numbers game, with only a sidelong glance at the surface waters, whose trade in fish once filled this port with sails.

Even when spring comes again and I watch the familiar, silvery bodies of the alewives coming in to spawn, I see them through a glass in which everything but the immediate foreground disappears into a distance, like the sea to which they will return. In spite of whatever facts and figures I have been able to pick up about them, the alewives swim off again into the silvery unknown, an image translated to me by my senses. Fish are so quick to live and quick to die that they seem to belong to another entirely different realm of experience, but that is one of the reasons I follow them. They help to keep me in touch with one of the magic realities of my surroundings. I think of them, for a good part of the year, as distinguished neighbors. Now I am never quite sure that they will come back again in the numbers that once lifted the living sea into inland waters.

The "sacred cod" of Massachusetts once ranged from the Gulf of Maine to Labrador. The specimens caught by local fishermen were very large — fifty to sixty pounds was not unusual. One codfish caught by a vessel off Georges Bank many years ago weighed in at 180 pounds. Cod were found from the surface down to at least 250 fathoms. They fed on sea urchins, sea cucumbers, crabs, shrimp, and lobsters. With their voracious appetite, they also preyed on small fish such as sand launces and capelin, as well as herring and squid. Old boots, old jewelry, fragments of rope and cloth were found in their stomachs. They produced a prodigious amount of eggs. The larvae and fry drifted in the currents until they sank to the bottom to grow to a more mature stage.

Serious declines in fish populations, especially in the ground fisheries dominated by the cod, have been made public for many years. A two-hundred-mile limit was put into place after factory ships of foreign nations such as Russia and Japan had been taking unprecedented numbers of fish and processing them on board. But in recent years, decline turned to disaster. Eighty percent of the codfish were gone off Labrador, Newfoundland, and the Gulf of St. Lawrence. Haddock, once a staple food off New England waters, had declined by 90 percent. The halibut was scarce, as well as the yellowtail flounder. In the Canadian maritime provinces, hundreds of fishing communities were affected. Fifty thousand fishermen were out of work and dependent on federal subsidies.

For centuries, fishing vessels from Europe, Canada, and the United States were in competition with local coastal fishermen from New England to Newfoundland. There were very few restrictions on these large vessels, no legal regulations, no government observers on board, and they could not be licensed within the three-mile limit. Most local people could find plenty not more than a day or two beyond their home ports. Every year the yield of fish was sustained. During the days of sail, the vessels were not very large, and they had not reached the point where the use of oil cut down on profits.

Following World War II, Canadian and U.S. fishing vessels, the trawlers and the draggers, began to be modernized. After a decline in ground fisheries became obvious, an effort was made to finance commercial fisheries in order to replenish the stock, an effort, in reality, that speeded up the decline. Draggers were built that were one hundred feet or more in length and equipped with the latest in electronic devices. It was now possible for operators to scan the ocean floor below them, not only to find fish populations, but also to estimate their size and extent. A modern dragger can tow a thirty-foot-wide net through water, taking everything in its path, and its pilot can then make a sharp 180-degree turn and reverse its direction. With this relentless, total method of fishing, the fish have nowhere to hide. The scale of killing and waste on these modern efficiency vessels is extravagant in the extreme. "Towed through the dense masses of fish such as spawning cod, draggers take everything. The captured fish are then hauled hundreds of feet to the surface in a few minutes. They blow up like balloons as their swim bladders inflate. Everything that reaches the surface after such an ordeal is dead."*

Along with tons of discarded, unmarketable fish, species such as puffins, shearwaters, porpoises, and even whales have been caught in the nets and killed. In an article in the *Maine Times* of November 8, 1993, Phyllis Austin reported that

---

Fisheries and Marine Policy Review of Canada, vol. 1, no. 2, St. John's, Newfoundland.

"the shrimp have been the most notorious for waste. Seventy-five percent that is dredged up may be discarded.

"Dr. Steve Murawski of the Northeast Fisheries Center at Woods Hole, Massachusetts, says that 'for every pound of shrimp caught three-quarters of a pound of fish has been discharged.'"

Modern technology, defeating its own purpose of ever-greater yield, has destroyed the most famous fishing grounds in the world. The idea that the Grand Banks and Georges Bank could be turned into ecological deserts was once un-thinkable, but it is a present-day reality. What the fishermen call "trash fish," such as dogfish or skate, now make up about 70 percent of the catch, and the great cod of history seems to be gone in any real quantity for the foreseeable future.

After a moratorium on ground fishing which was clearly not going to bring the fishing stocks back any time soon, the Canadian government put an outright ban on it in 1993. The licenses of fishermen to operate their boats were bought out, and they were given payments of some twenty-five to forty dollars a week. Many of the fifty thousand have joined the ranks of the unemployed. Fishing grounds of a vast complexity have been turned into underwater deserts. And not only the fish but a way of life is dying, one with an honorable history. It is as if the foundation of the live-lihood and lives of fishermen and their families had sud-denly dropped away beneath them.

I think of the Newfoundlander in his dory who, sur-rounded by his load of magnificent fish, waved to me many years ago, and I despair for him and our own loss of contact with the genuine riches of this world. In a cold, calculating market that sees living things in terms of profit and loss, we become detached from reality. The destruction of an entire marine ecosystem is met with apathy from the mass of us. If there is any solution to things it is always technology, backed by the "free enterprise system." Technology without feeling is one of the most violent and destructive forces on earth.

Fishermen were always independent-minded gamblers. They gambled on the changes in the weather and on the nature of their quarry, which was notorious for its appearances and disappearances over the centuries. But they knew the sea and its food which gave them their zest and fortitude. They were part of a neighborhood of the sea. The whole ocean has a tidal weight of its own which buoyed up those who wrestled their living from it for so many thousands of years. Without them, who is to tell us where to find the depths from which we came?

As the *Marine Policy Review of Newfoundland* so eloquently puts it: "In fisheries, as in many other areas, our technical ability and voraciousness for the world's natural resources have outstripped the ability of the Earth to regenerate the life of which we are an indivisible part."

It is as much of a calamity to lose the fishermen as it is to lose the fish. Fishing communities around the world have harbored the ways of the sea in themselves, a knowledge not soon acquired again after it, and they, have been abandoned.

The decline in fish populations, along with the destruction of marine ecosystems, is not confined to the east coast of North America, nor to the Pacific, where the halibut and salmon fisheries are in danger. The Black Sea and the Mediterranean have also suffered major declines in fish and in the health of their marine communities. Pollution, loss of habitat, and over-fishing are having world-wide effects. The industrial world assaults the earth's resources with all the thoroughness of starfish destroying a coral reef, but coral reefs regenerate after a period of time. It is as if we, with our techniques, our inventiveness, our vast oil supplies, and gigantic food markets, have become insensitive to the needs and dimensions of a nature which has always supported us. Have we become accustomed to the idea of extinctions? No Man's Lands are being created every day with casual ferocity. The power to live outside the provenance of the rest of creation is an emptiness of our own making.

In their book, *Beyond the Limits*, a sequel to *The Limits to Growth*, Donella H. Meadows, Dennis L. Meadows, and Jørgen Randers point out that it is not necessarily the people's fault that fish stocks are plummeting but that of the modern world and its state of mind:

Ecologist Paul Ehrlich once expressed surprise to a Japanese journalist that the Japanese whaling industry would exterminate the very source of its wealth. The journalist replied, "You are thinking of the whaling industry as an organization that is interested in maintaining whales; actually it is better viewed as a huge quantity of [financial] capital attempting to earn the highest possible return. If it can exterminate whales in ten years and make a 15% profit, but it could only make 10% with a sustainable harvest, then it will exterminate them in ten years. After that, the money will be moved to exterminating some other resource." (A friend of ours has heard a similar argument from a firm cutting tropical timber in Sabah.)

The market players who are busily exterminating resources are utterly rational. What they are doing makes complete sense, given the rewards and constraints they see from the place they occupy in the system. The fault is not with people, it is with the system. An unregulated market system governing a common resource inevitably leads to overshoot and the destruction of the commons. Only political constraints of some kind can protect the resource, and those political constraints are not easy to attain.

Fish were once equated with the River of Life. On the shores of the world where they were abundant, or as we would put it, of "economic importance," they were sometimes deified. It was essential they be propitiated. Religious rites were performed to insure their permanence. To the native tribes of our northwest coast, the salmon was a primary source of food, and because that great fish had appeared in the spring for time out of mind, it had a reputation for immortality. Since the migration of the "salmon people" was vital to man, it followed that they should not be offended, or they might not return from their homes in the sea. This required certain ritual observances, ceremonies following the salmon's own rites of life and death.

When I read in the back pages of a newspaper a few years ago that the upriver population of Coho salmon on the Columbia River was in danger of extinction, I thought it must be news of major importance. Yet it seems to have met with major indifference in "the media." Every year, those great fish make an epic journey for many miles into the Cascade Mountains. They were a symbol to me of the triumph of life and that they should suddenly disappear was as if the river itself were being deprived of its spirit. The courageous, resilient salmon, on both the Atlantic and Pacific, match the waterways of a continent. Besides the Coho, a number of other Pacific species have become seriously reduced in population during this century.

This decline cannot be attributed solely to human influence, although we have clearly added to the downward slide. When Lewis and Clark, on their journey up the Missouri, reached the northwest coast, they found Indian tribes starving from the lack of salmon. Over the centuries, such natural causes as volcanic disturbances, long periods of drought resulting in low water in the rivers, plus atmospheric changes brought on by great ocean currents such as El Nino, have resulted in low productivity. Overfishing since the nineteenth century has also produced marked declines. Massive dams, the rerouting of rivers, overuse of their water, and pollution have also had their effect. Modern offshore trawlers and gill nets have intercepted the salmon as they moved into river mouths. Disturbance of their ecosystems and the destruction of eggs and fry has been widespread.

Fish stocks, such as the cod, the haddock, and the West Coast halibut have been reduced almost to the point of no return. Small populations of fish, as is the case with other animals in reduced populations, are less able to maintain their cohesion. They are more prone to disease and genetic disorders. They are far less capable of competing with other species introduced by humans. The simplistic way in which the modern world, always out to beat the odds, stifles the ability of living systems to regenerate should serve as a dire warning to us. We too could reach the end of the line, but it never has been easy for us to stop. Losing the sense of a greater ecosystem in ourselves, we become deficient in awareness, detached from original dependence. Nature does not give us a free ride, but demands an entire commitment.

The great reproductive journey of the wild salmon, a migration that takes in hundreds of thousands of miles of open sea, is one of surpassing complexity, which mere numbers and statistics cannot solve. The great fishes are inhabitants of a profoundly mysterious realm which can never answer to the domination of a single race. They were nurtured by powers we try to imitate, but are unable to contain. If they are only numbers, a matter of profit and loss, rather than essential food, it will need a faith greater than ours to make them return.

Swallows
and Swallowtails

The summers I spend on the coast of Maine are not vacations, in the sense that I have no nine-to-five job to go back to or escape from. I am past the age, in any case. One advantage of retirement is that it gives you time to open yourself to your surroundings. There is always something that transcends the immediate. You seldom escape the pressures of our world and its murderous news (count no day lost in which you have no idea of what is going on), but there are other voices to listen to.

I dig and hoe in our admirable vegetable garden, while my wife makes admirable use of its products. I swim the nearby salt waters when they are warm enough and go out in the boat occasionally to check up on the seals or explore the rocky shores. Such days may sound uneventful, but all that time, which passes quickly, what I am really doing is trying to keep open to the unexpected. Who knows what miracles may lie in wait? Out of the tidal world that keeps rushing in and out below our house, out of the clouds in their endless transformations and the trees that hold the wind, come messages that could illuminate my existence.

In this I have had some help from the barn swallows, which keep me company in the barn where I try to write. They nest high over my head along the rafters under the barn roof. Even with an extension ladder the nests are hard to reach, so I am unable to take credit for any scientifically conducted research. I sit downstairs in a stall once meant for a horse, listening to their urgent business from a distance. Every morning, I open the barn door to hear the rapid twittering with which they keep in rhythmic communication. I find it cheerful and reassuring. Sharing space with swallows is a comfort in an age that is all too likely to be indifferent to their fate. As long-distance migrants, they are also a link between this barn and the oceanic space beyond it. And the intensity with which they follow through the season, win or lose, wakes me up to major changes in minor phenomena that I might otherwise ignore. They make this garden wilder than I realized.

One morning in June, when I was sitting in the barn trying to free my thoughts of their logjams, I happened to notice a black and yellow swallowtail butterfly hovering on the edge of the grape arbor outside. I guessed that it must be feeding on nectar from the flowers, so I walked out, peered under the leaves, and sniffed those clusters of tiny, yellow-green blossoms. Their scent was wonderfully sweet and delicate, and I did not remember ever having smelled them before. I suppose I have tended to think more of the grape than the process that leads up to it. Following swallows or swallowtails takes me on trails I have never walked. This is not only a question of gathering more information about natural history; it has to do with inner translations of an outer world.

The full-blown month of June brings in the fireflies, little flying lights blinking on and off, some quite close to the open ground, some above the treetops. I remember them in the Talamanca range of mountains in Costa Rica, where their light seemed twice as brilliant as it does in New England. They ringed the clearing where we spent the night like so many tribal fires before the dark mountain forest, where the now dispossessed Indians once prayed to the forest soul. During their courtship rituals, male fireflies use "flash patterns" to attract the females. Both sexes respond with acute sensitivity. These summer dances are not only a matter of connections between light organs and the nervous system. They are revelations of the powers behind all earth's behavior.

The summer before had been unusually hot and dry, with only showery intervals. That might have forced an abundance of flowers and fruit and accounted for many more butterflies than usual. I followed the dark little wood nymphs as they flitted across the fields, as well as fritillaries, painted ladies, monarchs, and others that came in closer to the garden. This was a new pursuit for me, and I only began to get a glimpse of their habits and characteristics. How long do they live? A month or so, a few weeks, a year and a half in the case of the famous monarch. Long enough to ensure their meetings with the plants they depend on for their existence, and at the right time. The timing seems perfect, and incalculable, a rhythmic expression of planetary change. When I pass a butterfly taking nectar from a flower, I am stopped in my tracks by the dynamics of the encounter. These interacting worlds make the length of life irrelevant. They defy mortality.

Later on, as August was passing by, a day of high wind and heavy rain filled dry streams with water. The next morning I felt something as light as a leaf drop down beside me, where it lay wedged between the grasses. At first, it looked to me as if one of our granddaughters had lost her thin, spangled bracelet. Then I realized that it was an eastern black swallowtail, with very torn wings. When I touched it, it made a few feeble efforts to fly up. I could see that there were sky-blue patches on its wings between a double band of white spots, and two coral-colored dots at the base of the tail, which had been worn down to almost nothing. As I walked away from that still beautiful remnant of life, a line from a great English poem I had once memorized came into my head: "Brightness falls from the air."

> Brightness falls from the air.
> Queens have died, young and fair.
> Dust hath closed Helen's eye.
> I am sick. I must die.
> Lord have mercy on us.

It is this ephemeral magic that outlasts us all.

The swallows were intently involved in a more acute sense of timing than I am capable of. I try to arrive early enough in the spring to open the barn window and let them in. In a protected site like a barn, their nesting season is relatively long as compared with that of a seabird like a tern, which is highly exposed to predation and whose nesting is often delayed by the weather. Red squirrels and an occasional rat may come into the barn to eat eggs or newly hatched chicks, but as a rule the birds are fairly safe. After the nests are built, the white, speckled eggs, up to five or six in a nest, incubate in roughly two weeks, and the young fly when they are eighteen to twenty-three days old. The nesting season is long enough for some swallows to lay two clutches of eggs and still be feeding their young in early September. After the young are fledged and leave the nest, the parents seem to go on feeding them for a few days. Then off the birds go toward the southern hemisphere, migrating fairly low over coastal waters, occasionally to be struck down by storm waves or drowned at sea.

A bird's nest is often thought of as an expendable, temporary platform on which the young are hatched out and reared for a short time, and which is then abandoned to the weather. A nest is not a permanent home in our sense of the term, though heaven knows we are disrupting our homes to the extent that nothing on this planet seems permanent. But the barn swallow, like that "sea swallow" the tern, which nests on an outer line of dunes, is a long-distance memorizer. The swallows often return to the very spot they nested in the year before. This habit implies ancient, built-in skills of navigation, a sense of geographical distinctions, and a remarkably close-knit relationship with the atmosphere. It amounts to a long-range confidence we are sorely lacking. Look into a bird's nest and you will find a true home, which can never betray the earth in which it is located.

Lazy clouds, their bellies gray with moisture, move by but drop no rain. I hear the incoming tide rushing through the inlet below the house. The vast night moves in again, with its own brilliant star travelers. The swallows are quiet in the barn, while the fireflies still flash their messages to each other over open ground.

The adult swallows are increasingly active after the young hatch out, constantly moving out over the waters along the shore or over inland fields, and skipping back through the open window with the thousand of insects they catch. I can now see several nests with unfledged, naked young, their little heads waggling up as they beg for food. In a week or so they are almost feathered out. The bigger they grow, the more they crowd their nest, until their white bellies show over the rim. On the first day of July, two juveniles are perched on the ridge of the barn roof outside, eagerly waiting to be fed. The adults fly up to give them a fleeting bite of food they carry in their bills. Other times, they whisk by as if to encourage the young to follow after them as they chase insects. The parents fly higher or lower, depending on atmospheric conditions. When the air is dense with fog and mist without enough wind to blow them away, the insects fly low, and on a clear day, much higher. Countrymen, with some justice, used to think of swallows as indicators of coming rain. They were also widely associated with water, for their habit of feeding over it, even on migration. In ancient times, swallows were fertility symbols, and because of their early arrival are still thought of as the forerunners of spring.

It rains all night, after weeks of drought. In the morning, a soft wind blows from the west. On the ebb tide, at low water when a fringe of muddy shore is opened up, three yellowlegs arriving early from arctic nesting grounds fly in to land on the shore and just as quickly fly up and away again. An occasional osprey circles overhead, trying to spot a fish. When the waters of the sea flood in through the outer islands, the long strands of the eelgrass begin to lift and reverse direction, and the golden rockweed swings with the tide. The great, controlled volume of the ocean hangs in the offing while its waters fan out with a full freight of sunlight.

The tide moves in and out below our house with mathematical regularity. I read the familiar signs of passing summer in the leaves of the trees and in the sequence of the flowers. An increasing number of shorebirds now stop by on their way south from their nesting grounds in the arctic. I think all the plants and animals are more literate at reading a continent than I am. I also believe that we give them too little credit for being principal actors in this changing year. The barn swallows, now beginning to feel the need to move out, are possessed of an accurate inner sense of distance that puts mine to shame. We know what flyways they take on their migration, how long it lasts, and where they are likely to end up, but we are still on the outside looking in. It is as if we were losing a corresponding sense of direction in ourselves which we once had without trying. It is not through conscious knowledge and information alone that we follow these great annual passages, but through that restless spirit that will always be a child of the unknown.

Just outside and below the upstairs window of our house, asphalt shingles cover the roof of a one-room annex. It is a very hot day, but a number of newly fledged swallows plus a few adults crouch down there on the asphalt, as the temperature climbs toward ninety degrees. Their dark little eyes seem glazed over with pleasure. I can watch them through the window from only a few feet away, listening to their warbly chatter, hearing what seems only a string of tonalities, though it probably contains points of emphasis beyond my discerning. It is like an extended music in the air. The land around me gathers a range of music I have hardly begun to translate.

I notice, incidentally, that when these sunbathers spread out their tails they reveal white spots on them like the spots on butterfly wings. Such distantly related signals fascinate me. To look down on swallows as beings of narrow focus is to cut earth's wings and fill the earth with emptiness. I am only glad I have them here to look down on me.

Their blue-black feathers with a hint of purple, together with their cinnamon breasts, suggest burnt metal, smoke, and fire. Swallows were once thought to be fire-bringers, which goes well with their connection with water. After the biblical Flood, which extinguished all fires on earth, they brought fire back from heaven. According to Edward Armstrong's *The Folklore of Birds*, the swallow "shares honors with the wren, for it is said that when the swallow was fetching fire from heaven a hole was burnt in its tail, but the wren seized the fire and brought it to earth at the cost of losing its own feathers."

To the Sioux, the swallow is the *akacita*, messenger of the terrible Thunderbird behind the mountains, where the yellow sun goes down to rest. This is the violet-green swallow, similar to what we know in the East as the tree swallow. Out on the Great Plains, when thunderheads mass before the distant hills in late afternoon, these swallows race back and forth hunting insects, and you know the birds carry messages of the earth's spirit.

On the sixteenth of August, sixty more swallows put in an appearance, having finished their nesting in some other part of this coastal range. They fly around for a few hours and roost on the barn with the others. Then these early migrants disappear. After dark I notice there are very few fireflies left. The responsive world is moving on at its ancient, rhythmic pace, leaving me to catch up as best I can.

During the early weeks of August, two nests are occupied by chicks not quite ready to move out. In the growing quiet of the barn, they are still being fed by the parents. The original population is down to a few.

On August twenty-third, we encountered a wonderful sight as we walked out of the front door into an afternoon bathed in dazzling light. Through it a great swarm of dragonflies was speeding in all directions, masterfully turning tight corners as they attacked all flies in the vicinity. Their colors of terra-cotta, red, and yellow glinted in the light. They were like a troop of bold, costumed warriors on a sudden raid. I guessed them to be globe-trotters, which have been known to travel as far as three hundred miles out to sea. I had no net, but it might have done me no good. These dragonflies are very hard to catch. They have broad wings and spectacular eyesight, which enables them to see an insect far out ahead of them as well as close at hand. I had no idea where they came from. I now remember this as one of the most brilliant moments of the year. To hear that in many parts of the country dragonflies like these are becoming endangered or extinct because of the pollution of the waters in which they breed has implications for our own sight. Our vision grows dimmer with their demise.

On the twenty-fourth, as I have it in my notes, a cold front has moved in on a north wind. The next day there are still some twenty swallows left on the ridge of the barn, and they are joined during the day by six more. They keep flitting out over the waters of the shore and returning. About seven-thirty in the evening, as darkness falls, some move into the barn to spend the night. These few, now seven or eight, are the last of the original flock. In the morning there are two young ones left, perched on top of the barn. They seem to be waiting to be fed, but no parent puts in an appearance, and after an hour or two they are gone. That outward motion in them, as in their tribe, is irresistible. All is quiet in the barn until another year.

𝒥 took a quotation from *Victory*, Joseph Conrad's novel, the other day, in which he wrote about the era of colonial empire in the tropics: "These white men looked on native life as a mere play of shadows—a play of shadows the dominant race could walk through unaffected and disregarded in the pursuit of its incomprehensible aims." We have nearly obliterated the shadows, occupying our native land almost as if it did not exist. Our aims seem even more incomprehensible than theirs.

Habits of power and domination pursue us, but the reality is that we do not rule. We only try to do so, out of fear and confusion. Still, the native, traditional values, which underlie the enduring society of swallows as well as human beings, give us what stability we can claim. We are unable to desert the seasons and their living signals, their illuminations under the sun, without casting ourselves into limbo, a darkness of our own making.

We may be returning to a companionship with poverty, or what we have put down as insignificant. This is the level of truth, among lives that never shared our pretensions to superiority. Since we occupied this continent, we have respected very little that is not property. But only to possess is no distinction. As I have discovered, you learn most from all you do not own.

The messengers of water, fire, and fertility fly under the passing clouds, none of which are adequately described by the weather reports. It is our inner weather we should be attending to. The outer world that is our present obsession sacrifices the inner one to illusions of power, and we lose our bearing, become ignorant of ourselves.

I join a wind I am unable to control. I am out on the passionate waters, which are tumbling in and tumbling out on a rip tide, erasing centuries of human violence and despair, under the somersaults of the sun, on its omnipotent journey.

The fog moves in out of the far horizon, out of the world-wandering seas, the tidal lungs of the globe heaving out and drawing in like our own, while the rivers of the continent trace earth's circulation.

My small boat sits over the swirling waters, waiting for forever to happen all over again. Under us, the wild, silver-sided fishes roam in search of food, the plankton twitch and swirl, all of them dancers and functionaries on this vast stage of tidal being as it travels through the universe.

Birds in Space

$\mathscr{A}$nother summer is speeding by, and the barn has been full of swallows again. A baby bird, newly hatched, has been pitched out of its nest for some unknown reason, and lies on the barn floor below, still feebly struggling. Because I have no idea which nest it came from, I am unable to put it back. It is past rescue, past hope, as it has been every nesting year for countless young ones, victims of accident, predation, or of lack of food.

This tiny, naked bird is blue-black in color, except for a pinkish smudge on its breast, which would have changed, in a startlingly short time, to an adult's bold, burnished-bronze band of feathers. After a few weeks of chasing after their parents, and learning to fend for themselves, returning to the barn but gradually moving farther out, the young swallows disappear altogether. They learn to join the general migration, following many days of exercise in touch-and-go and fast maneuver. A swallow on the wing is a test of superior agility. The young will fly off to a southern continent they have never seen before, but the way is known, their route an ancient inheritance. Rational interpretation has never quite solved the mysteries of migration, but if it is so simple to the migrants that they leave without hesitation, it may be that we have been neglecting some equivalent mystery in ourselves. We stay behind the birds, desperately trying to locate ourselves, all over the place, as if there were no permanence anywhere.

This barn in Maine, where the swallows have nested every year since I opened the back window to the loft about thirty years ago, is only a remnant of the original structure. That burned down, I believe, in the 1940s. It was the focal point of a saltwater farm that originated in the mid-eighteenth century. At the corner of the field above the barn, which slopes down to the shore, is what the country people called a "sheep bier," a stone wall enclosure of the kind the farmers built in the British Isles. The enclosure is still visible, but the trees, balsam fir and white pine, have long since taken hold within it. Its stone walls have fallen in and are covered by leaves and forest duff, so that the original outlines are hard to find. It was once suggested to me that if I dug deep enough I might be able to find some eighteenth-century coins and artifacts there, but all I was able to uncover was the nest of a red squirrel. These scampering, scolding, pretty little animals often move to our house during the winter when we are absent, caching seeds from the white pines in various hiding places about the house, and occasionally using beds and furniture for their nests. Unlike rats and mice, they do not eat whatever food we may have left behind us, and the minor damage they do does not prompt me to declare all-out war against them. It is their habit, as it is with people, to be tempted by houses left empty and to move into them. Several hundred miles to the south, on Cape Cod, these active animals, original inhabitants of the northern forests, seem to have been greatly reduced in population. I suspect this has to do with a very large number of gray squirrels which have pushed them out, in an area that has been steadily turning into suburbia.

The swallows also moved in, with our encouragement, and have been returning for some thirty years. In the absence of horses and cows and of much agriculture except for our small vegetable and flower garden, the swallows have brought a new and useful form of employment to the barn. I do not simply tolerate them. They bring another life dimension to keep me company. I have been asked how I can endure their droppings all over the rafters and the barn floor, especially since these are of little value as compared to cow and horse manure. Yet swallows are no more "dirty" than we are, and in many respects much cleaner. They are with us only for a few months, and during that time they don't share space with cars, for obvious reasons. It is my opinion that cars should be left outside, in company with as much dirt and danger as may be permitted on the highway.

Barn swallows are familiar enough, but like many long-distance migrants they are like visitors from foreign lands, with a strange quickness and intensity in their habits that seems to make short work of time as we conceive of it. To have these long-distance runners with me helps unstick me from an obsession with our closed and relentless society. They answer to a different pace, and to different summons from the sun and moon. Even in the short phrases of their "vocalizing" which indicate certain discernible, emotional states having to do with alarm, aggression, sources of food and direction, they are not less limited than I am, but in contact with a more exposed world than I am capable of interpreting. The outer world may pull them away and return them over thousands of miles, but in their traveling minds they know their way. They can recognize this coastal world in its tidal changes out of long acquaintance. They help to center me in their geography.

Bird talk is not small talk, but a language, or languages, pared down to essential meanings. What they are able to express seems highly limited from our perspective but lies in deep with other electric response and eloquence in the worlds of life. We are coming around belatedly to concede that other animals may share in the great realm of consciousness, and even use conscious thought to accomplish their ends, if not to such an advanced and complex extent as the human mind. Yet a bird in its closeness to the elements, and to the tides of the atmosphere, is probably more aware than we are of the subtle shifts and changes in its surroundings. There is a sentient intelligence in birds that is not continually distracted by its own power and sense of possession. Their mastery of the great air is in every move they make.

It is mid-August. So far as I can tell, there are only three active nests left out of the original twenty, and the young swallows in them are fledged and ready to move out. After dark I go into the barn on a minor errand. I do not hear a sound. The silence is eloquent. I have to turn on the electric light, a bulb in the ceiling, to see where I am and to find whatever object I am looking for. But in this great silence I hear the nights of all the world. How profoundly these birds know and obey it. The tides outside are smoothly running by. I hear them when I leave the barn, but they are only a water drop in eternity. I turn off the light, feeling unutterably clumsy with my human pretensions. But outside a limitless silence, protector of all nurture, fills the world, and the Milky Way, glittering with stars, crosses the universe like an immense sash.

This complete silence, fostered in their children by Indian mothers crossing hostile territory, and instinctively understood by nestling birds, has no relation to enforced security and protection. The silence of the starry places calls all things to its measure of truth.

Subject to the restless dynamics of the world ocean, this Maine shore extends to all others. The marine organisms that live on every level of the tidal zones, and in the waters beyond them, each with its singular identity, are part of a fluid, multiple association. Simply because each species coexists with other communities in a nonexacting world of change and exposure, there is a sense in which they elude the categories we apply to them. It is not surprising that someone should spend a lifetime on the sexual conduct of a flea, or on the particulars of a snail's migration. No life is entirely insignificant that belongs to earth's magnitudes.

Landscapes that are conceived as being totally possessed by our civilization begin to lose their ability to sustain us. When we conceive of them only in terms of how much money they can bring, they cannot be seen for what they are as resolutions of surpassing complexity. When the fish disappear as a result of our exploitation of them, so do the native skills of a fisherman. When populations of birds or other "wildlife" begin to decline at an alarming rate, they leave great wastelands in space, which we, becoming used to loss, hardly notice. If birds are only numbers rather than beings, they can vanish with hardly a trace of them left in our minds.

"Instant communication," which can carry anyone's messages anywhere in almost no time flat, is a method of creating order out of potential chaos in an overcrowded world. Time shrinks. Space is overcome. And so we are translated beyond locality and the time needed to experience its own language through living, experience, and accommodation. The world we cannot see and listen to every hour of every day is now filled with one voice that continually grows in volume, and deafens our living rooms.

So I go down to the water's edge again, to listen for my neglected ancestors, whose voices sound in the trees and carry across the shore with the mewing of the gulls. There is a great, innovative music out there which we are sadly neglecting. The inner earth is a song I have only started to listen to.

On many summer days the fog may bank up over the horizon with a gray deliberation. Then it begins to drift in across the rocky ledges and through the dark, upward spiraling spruce trees ranked thickly together on the islands. The morning air is full of fine water droplets. The wind picks up. The sun shines through and the fog begins to dissipate. I travel out in our skiff and trail my fingers in the water, which feels as smooth as velvet. I hear the sharp cry of a tern and suddenly several of them come floating in out of the distance like speeding clouds. They have now finished their nesting season on some small, outer island. They cruise in low over the surface, scanning it for schools of small fish. Then each one pauses, circles in the air, hovers for a few seconds and makes a slanting dive, hitting the water with an audible "chock." If they catch a fish, they speed away with it in their bills. This life exercise has an almost metronomic beat. It is an accomplished skill which has served terns well over thousands of years of natural attrition and adversity. But along these shores the triumphant crying of the terns has become dimmer.

During the past century, following a relentless persecution of terns, egrets, and shorebirds by market gunners, there came a massive intrusion by a growing urban population. The gulls, taking advantage of its wastes, increased by leaps and bounds. They forced tern colonies off their islands and robbed unprotected nests of their eggs and sometimes chicks. Once the terns nested on favorable islands offshore by the hundreds of thousands, but they have been reduced to a comparative few. Strict conservation measures, with the vigilant protection of a few key islands, have kept their numbers from further decline. When these immaculately feathered birds drift by me, and I hear their strident calls, I know them not as a threatened species but as winners, out of the endless history of the seas in all their changing fire and passion.

On one part of the local shore which I have passed many times in our boat, looking for seals or seabirds, there is a pile of rocks, carefully placed one on top of the other, for reasons unknown to me. From offshore, this pile looks to me like a seated man, with his arms folded across his knees. The topmost rock looks a little like a Mayan or Aztec headdress, giving this rock man a mythical cast. He may have been sitting there fifty years ago, and he may still be there fifty years from now, an impartial observer of past, present, and future. He makes nothing of dates, or the ages of man. He is present at all the birthdays of the world.

Out of the fringe of spruce and pine, the tangle of wild

raspberry, and clearings of hay-scented fern, behind the rock man's back, there comes the hauntingly beautiful song of the white-throated sparrow. Its notes are clear, lilting and tremulous, the tones of all forest mornings from long ago and far away. When I was young, I was told that it said: "Sam Peabody, Peabody, Peabody." But it may be that old Sam's farm has gone, like so many others, and his descendants scattered across the continent. Perhaps "Oh Canada, Canada, Canada" is more appropriate, in recognition of the great band of coniferous forests this bird still inhabits.

One day as I was making my way through the undergrowth I flushed a white-throat up off of the ground ahead of me, from where it had a hidden nest under a fallen limb. There were four lightly speckled eggs in it, of a pale, greenish blue, fitting the greenish light that fell in from the shimmering evergreens. So one perfection complements another and answers to the sky.

There is nothing more exalting to be heard than the flute-like spiraling notes of the hermit thrush rising out of a forest slope. The song seems to measure the immeasurable. I have always associated certain wooded places, fields, or watersides with the songs I've heard there. The voice of a veery or a wood thrush in the evening down by the lake where I used to live hangs in my memory as imperishable, sounding for a special quality inherent in the land. The land itself has a long memory to which its various voices respond, each in its own fashion. That is why the land may still come back after apparent oblivion.

Bird songs have a direct relationship with location. Charles Hartshorne, in his book *Born to Sing*, pointed out that the strongest and most musical singers are those forced to rely more on sound than on sight. Treetop songs sound less clear and resonant than those issuing out of under-growth where the singers are often invisible, simply because those which feed and nest near the ground have need for better acoustical signals than the singers high overhead on the trees.

Ever since I first began to hear a hermit thrush singing out of a hillside, hidden from view, I have tried to stop, look, and listen for the qualities of things unseen. The songs of the white-throat or of the hermit thrush rise out of the true proportions of space. The birds sing of an imperishable forest. They inherit the memories of their race, and I believe the land itself has a memory. Intellectual and material ascendancy is not for them.

The song of a hermit thrush is known to be part of a courtship ritual in which two males compete with each other through the intensity of their voices for a small portion of territory. The loser withdraws, leaving the field to its rival. So song suits order and right relationships in the place appropriate to it.

Along with the meistersingers, there are also ventriloquists. I was once deceived by an ant thrush in the rain forest of Costa Rica into thinking it was a hundred yards away when it suddenly appeared almost at my feet. This was after I had been whistling for it, in a fair imitation of its voice, which had made it circle around me at a near distance. This response and interchange was enchanting. I have also listened to startling imitations of other birds by the mockingbird, catbird, and brown thrasher. In Greenland I came across a large group of ravens conversing on a hillside, with an extraordinary range of sounds, from harsh, guttural exclamations to whistles, clicks, and even warbles.

The ornithologists call this "vocalization," as compared

with human speech and its conscious use of words, but it may be closer to a language than we give it credit for. As I listened, in any case, I felt as if I were present at a parley or communal meeting of these great black birds which originated in the very ancient world behind them.

There are many birds that have very little vocal ability, and all you seem to hear are passing comments with little apparent intention behind them. Until recently, I was never aware that the ruby-throated hummingbird had any "song" at all. One day in early August, as I was startled by a loud almost motorlike humming only a yard or so from my ear, there was a ruby-throat sipping nectar from a red nasturtium flower in a pot. As it hovered next to me I heard squeaky twittering. The next day, as I was sitting in a porch chair, that tiny, brilliant bird came at me like a flash from around the corner of the house. We met each other, eye to eye, but in a split second it changed course and sped away. I was wearing a red shirt at the time, and since these birds have an affinity for the color, I supposed it had mistaken me for a flower, a compliment I did not have the time to refuse.

The dynamics of a hummingbird's flight, as well as its habits, have been zealously studied. The ruby-throat's heart normally beats at five hundred times a minute when at rest, but during periods of intense activity the rate can increase to one thousand beats a minute. Its wings beat anywhere from sixty to two hundred times a second. On its migrations to Mexico and Central America, where it winters, it travels at some twenty-four miles an hour. It can fly backward as well as forward, and even upside down. Watching them feeding on a bank covered with jewelweed, before their departure in September, I felt that I had been introduced to an epic of creation. They are translations of immortal energy into art. With such an endowment, who needs a loud voice?

Even in its reduced state, what we call "the environment," as if we were its sole owners, is governed by complex alliances of dissimilar forms of life, true adventurers in the long tides of earth history. The voices in nature answer to the allowances of space. Even along those shores hemmed in by development, and almost crowded beyond the land's capacity, they can still be heard. The shrill, coughing bark of the fox sounds in the darkness. The coyote, constantly alert for everything in its surroundings, slips invisibly through the thickets. The waiting, watchful gulls send out their musical calls over the sound of the waves. The motion of all seasons is in their minds. Their senses are alert. They listen, knowing that the earth attends to its own. They were native Americans long before we outsiders gave the continent its name.

At regular times of the day, we can watch the vapor trails of passenger jets as they head in from Europe, on their computerized flight paths. But during the course of the seasons, during the day, and at times on a clear night, the winged migrants follow their own more fluid ways across the sky. They are the true internationalists, on the earth's missions. We can only guess where many of them came from, like the black-bellied plovers that gather on offshore rocks in late summer, down from the arctic. All of them, from the warblers that flit through the woods of spring to the sea ducks coming in or departing for various points of the compass, have the effect of centering us in what is still, for us in our insularity, an untraveled globe. Open landscapes, free for wanderers, are the ones best known. They are not known through human brain power alone, or an isolated ownership, but through those which carry the lands' still uncharted reaches in their minds.

One day I spotted a small, closely knit flock of snow geese flying very high overhead. I had seen large numbers of these magnificent birds in September, years ago, as they were resting and feeding in the St. Lawrence estuary not far from Quebec. They are high-altitude birds, without benefit of machinery. The barheaded goose flies regularly at thirty thousand feet to cross the high peaks of the Himalayas. I wonder, aside from what science may have found to account for this ability, whether it might not translate into an altitude of awareness. I suspect the geese know the waves of the atmosphere in a far less detached way than we do.

Modern man has so neutralized the lands he lives in that he can no longer find himself there, driving over the surfaces he has made toward random destinations. The continent with all its shining and shadowed motions sanctioned by the sun, calls us in. It is almost, these days, as if we had refused admission. It has become an act of will to join in on its own terms.

I was early on enchanted and tempted on by the world of birds, but I had not seen them clearly as societies, each structured differently according to need and to the world places they occupied, from the desert to the forest to the sea. They were not legitimate, as my own world seemed to view them, except as we granted legitimacy to them . . . which only meant that we were half-blinded to their very existence. We could cast them away at will. So it was that I was compelled out of a lagging indifference, implanted in me by my education, to look to the birds for insight into a world of awareness it had sadly neglected. This meant that

I yearned for the spaces they occupied in their own right. I had a feeling that the charts and maps we had engineered were only for our own use. Let nothing else apply. So I began to be pulled in to congresses, rituals, ceremonies, articulations I never knew existed before, civilizations created, and that is not too large a world for living communities so deeply engaged with the earth in all its detail.

We deny a planetary equity when we hold off its living things at arm's length, as if they, not being us, were less knowing in the ways of earth. We suffer from a terrible insularity, that tends to crowd out all distinction. I wrote a book about the terns, and I still do not know half enough about them. If we do not really know through what "mechanism" they find their way over immense distance to reach their territories, why should we think that we ourselves know where we are, or for that matter who we are. If I had more years to do it in, I would follow them as far as I can, to discover more lifesaving extensions in myself.

The tides of spring are flowing in again, not in any simple and flowery way, but with increasing light and intensity. Wet snow and ice fall in from the sky. Ice melts in the rivers, the lakes, and streams. Salamanders begin to circle in vernal pools, coaxed out of winter torpor into a mating dance. The ancient chorus of the hylas, or "spring peepers," rises from the cold water of the bogs to cry out to the stars. This is no Communications Enterprise to stifle the senses with its enormity. Leaf buds and the eyes of fish respond to the new light. Sea travelers fly in toward the shore. Others move on, winging toward the north.

On Cape Cod, where we spend the rest of the year after

leaving Maine, we own a small field below the house. On its edges there is a fringe of trees and thickets, now regenerating after centuries in which most of the woodlands were cut down. Tender leaves are unfolding into spring tapestries of light green, yellow, and pink. Various birds appear in what becomes an almost tropical abundance. A warbler, newly arrived from Central America, whisks in to explore a leaf, and as quickly drops and lifts away. A male towhee with a black bib perches high on an overhanging oak uttering low notes of alarm as I walk by. Chickadees race and bounce through the undergrowth with characteristic energy, while two brilliantly colored cardinals chase after each other through the trees. I hear the loud "wheep" of a great-crested flycatcher. They are all drawn in to join the intense engagements of the sun. They see detail which is invisible to me unless I happen to chance upon it, after much searching. They are the spring's explorers and adventurers, aware of subtleties in this landscape which we bury or ignore. This was only a "worthless woodlot" when I bought it. Its current value has now risen to a point of absurdity, but without relation to its value under the sun's authority. The exploiters now get the most money out of a land that has been cleaned up, which means that it has been deprived of its variety. But there is no holding back in this small wooded edge, engaged in the real work of the world on every level. All here are members of the greater community of light. If the birds, the insects, plants, and leaves now moving through this multiple engagement have no rights within our system, then we ourselves become closed out, unexceptional in the universe of life.

A Faire Bay

In about 1939 or 1940, I was riding on a train between New York City and Washington, D.C., idly looking out the window at the passing landscape full of industrial plants and then scattered houses and open fields. I heard the man in the seat behind me lamenting all the open spaces that were going to waste, as if they were missing parts of a jigsaw puzzle that should be entirely built by human effort. As one who had been brought up with open fields, and also because we were traveling through one of the most densely populated corridors in the nation, I felt very much annoyed. Later on, the thought came to me that my fellow traveler was simply an American idealist. His ideal was Progress, expressed in terms of smoking factories and busy towns from coast to coast. He believed in a right to expand, embracing the notions that fueled Daniel Webster's earlier speeches in the heady days of "westward the course of empire."

Although the "great open spaces" set the American dream on fire, progress was slow enough at first to accommodate land and nature. But it was our intention that the lands should accommodate us in all that we wanted from them. Still land and nature held their own, no longer wilderness but still full of space that was only partially settled, enough to cultivate local understanding.

Following World War I and a surge in population, Progress turned into Growth, which began to take on the characteristics of an avalanche. It was now a world of megalithic trade, one that looked back at settled, landed places with nostalgia, but one in which substitute illusions were manufactured every hour of the day. The reality was a homelessness that spread across the globe.

Ahead of our train was the Chesapeake, one of the major bays of the world, a great natural engine of exchanging waters and land. To early settlers it seemed inexhaustible in its natural riches, a place to live in for a thousand years. The great rivers whose waters ran into it and then out to the sea were handy arteries of commerce. The inner, native world of such a bay was one of rich and complex interchange. Its produce grew from the confluence of major rivers and a warm, temperate climate, and its local as well as migrant fish and birds shared in oceanic tides.

Industrial development and the growth of cities began to poison the arteries with human waste and chemicals. Grasses died, fish populations dwindled, the Chesapeake began to shrink. General possessions and universal property rights were overriding the freedom of the waters. The land was governed by absentee owners, who may have never seen or touched it. With the abandonment of natural law, the people began to lose their grasp of essential detail. They began to lose track of where their food came from. The human world was subjected to an unending stream of information which had little substance and ignored the land. The energies which might have been channeled into an exchange with the natural universe and all its societies was being spent on trying to control human disorders. Communication and Utility are overriding goals in our world, but nothing truly useful is ever accomplished without love.

So it is that the people who really know the Chesapeake, working night and day to "Save the Bay," are fully aware of its own original place in themselves. We cannot fly away from the great centers the earth has provided. They are permanently embodied in the land's first inheritors, fish, birds, crabs, oysters, grass, and trees, which can speak to us of what lasts and is not ephemeral, in greater exchanges of a universe of motion.

Unbridled growth is constantly running up against the limits of resources, and is at the point of no return. We are engaged in an experiment, if it can be called that, of disengagement from an earth to which we owe our own creation. Yet we can never be completely dematerialized from where we live. Refuse our attachment, and invite estrangement, even from ourselves. Those people whose homes and places of origin have been buried by an earthquake or lie under a major flood often insist on returning to where their houses or shelter once stood. Position and inner proportion are still as much alive in us as are the stations of the sun. This is a visceral as well as spiritual lodging. When violated, it can result in the unleashing of passionate violence and war. We can know where we ought to be without those illusions of omnipotence and self-sufficiency that beset us. We cannot expropriate the ancient depths of nature in ourselves. We were never above the land, or superior to it, any more than we are superior to the rest of nature. We are its dependents.

"Pull down thy vanity," said the poet to himself, as he landed in jail.

"A Faire Bay" was written for "Music of the Spheres," a group under the direction of flutist Katherine Hay and Frances Thompson McKay. It was read to music composed by Frances McKay entitled "Rites of Passage," and played at St. Mark's Episcopal Church in Washington, D.C., in the fall of 1987.

It is, said Captain John Smith, ". . . a faire Bay
compassed but for the mouth with fruitful and
delightsome land. Within is a country that may have
the prerogative over the most pleasant places of Europe,
Asia, Africa or America, for large and pleasant navigable
rivers. Heaven and earth never agreed better to frame a
place for man's habitation."

Out of the waters of the Chesapeake came a wilderness
store of food—oysters, crabs and clams, unending schools
of fish; and in the glistening marshes where waterfowl fed
on smartweed, wild celery and widgeongrass, sea lettuce
and eel grass, were river otter, muskrat, beaver and mink.
Gentle, shallow waters along a shoreline of four thousand
miles seemed to invite the world in to share its riches.
And the Susquehanna and its great estuary flowed with
a primal energy founded in the vast, still unknown
continent behind them.

It was a tidal world in motion, never the same, as
we ourselves have been in motion ever since we found it,
taking all we could to satisfy our needs. But can we take
so much that we become strangers to the Bay? Will the
fishing ruin the fishermen, and the harvest of the rivers
die? Can we subdue and conquer these great waters
beyond their capacity to receive us?

Where the Chesapeake lies under the mists of dawn,
or opened out to sunlight-shattered waters, its surface
falls and rises, inhaling, exhaling, like the lungs of the
living world.

The Bay is a state of being, a great heart pulsing
with the tides, exchanging sea and river water in
its veins.

Twice a day the sea mounds in and rolls its free length up
the Bay. Twice a day great water masses mix and change,
as river waters run toward the sea.

In this body is the earth's desire. The fishes and the
plankton suspended in its depth respond to beauties of
transformation, everlasting change. Storms pass over them
and they abide.

Now the thunder rolls, and pounds the great *tympanum*
of the Bay. Low and heavy it rolls and rumbles.
Lightning swells and flashes over the long, low shores,
and flying sheets of rain fall in out of violent darkness
with a wind whose spirit strips the trees.

So the Chesapeake has felt the hurricanes
across its giant back, in their wild screaming—
boats scattered and sunk, trees uprooted,
islands washed away . . .
in that fury the outer seas unleash,
born of the world ocean and its invincible demands,
moving in with judgments past undoing.

The mighty Susquehanna, empowered by a hurricane,
rising on the flood,
once drove the sea back
farther than living memory;

but the sea returns for its unending
conflict and collusion with the river.

The storm is over. The clouds clear off
toward that everlasting blue
which is the testament of vision,
the breeding ground of hopes and dreams;
and everything on earth prays to the sun.

"Life is a pure flame, and we live by the invisible sun
within us."
                                        —Sir Thomas Browne

Every cove, inlet and marsh, each creek and river has its
own distinction, known to every life that seeks it out.
Here is the wildness we rejected, the food we still
demand, the oysters and the clams, the crabs and fish that
were also the food of the people who lived with this land,
in intimate dependency, thousands of years before we
came, and gave their now legendary names to the rivers of
the Chesapeake: Wicomico, Rappahanock, Choptank,
Potomac, Poconoke.

"We always had plenty; our children never cried
from hunger, neither were our people in want. . . .
The rapids of the River furnished us with an abundance
of excellent fish, and the land being very fertile,
never failed to produce good crops of corn, beans,
pumpkins, and squashes. . . . Here our village
stood for more than a hundred years, during all of which
time we were the undisputed possessors of this

region. . . . Our village was healthy and there was no place in the country possessing such advantages, nor hunting grounds better than those we had in possession. If a prophet had come to our village in those days and told us that the things were to take place which have since come to pass, none of our people would have believed him."*

River water streaming and coiling in its abundance,
backtracking, pausing, running to the sea—
Out on the great Bay the passion of rip tides pulling
at the boats, rifting human balance and releasing it—
This energy and fury, and innate calm,
the bold dignity of waters running their own free way,
while the life within them
holds under the distant magnets of earth and sky.
Do we not belong here? Can we return?

White fog settles in over the shining grasses,
and tired boats, tethered to pilings,
lie on their own shadows.
Tidewaters gulp, and unseen fishes splash.
There is a whisper in the wind
over a deeper silence, where we might remember
being born.

Oh Chesapeake, how can we forget your marshes with their tidal swirling in our ears, and their inclusion of the multitudinous facets of light? These are sacred channels,

*Ma-ka-tai-me-she-kia-kiak, or Black Hawk, Chief of the Sioux and the Fox. From *Touch the Earth*, compiled by T. C. McLuhan.

keeping the tidal rise and fall of birth and death in an
eternal balance.

When showers pass and clouds blow by, the
"Johnny Crane," holding its yellow spear in readiness,
reflects sky blue upon its wings.

While in a warm hour the frogs are croaking with the
voice of water, a slim egret, with pure white wings and
body like a shell, lifts from tall grasses with a snoring cry.

In September, the young menhaden flip and turn their
silver bodies in the shallow river winding through the
marsh. How beautiful the fishes, every tribe with its
precious distinction, white perch, yellow perch, shad
and alewives, the slim young catfish and the striped bass.
They have tracings on their skin of water's varying light,
delicate and unequaled markings. Fishes lift the human
spirit out of isolation.

To fill and lay waste the marshlands, to deliver them
unto degradation, is to lose our own protection.
They shelter origins, and the earth requires them.

Out beyond the channeled grasses, across the spreading
waters, the winds are chasing an immortal distance.

The colonists came in from everywhere, around the
compass, around the clock, settling into these generous
shores; and they shot the deer, treed coons, stewed
squirrels or snapping turtles for dinner, trapped beaver
and muskrat, fished the rivers and raised corn and

tobacco. They warred with nature and enjoyed its fruits.
Canoes, punts and piraguas, bateaux and barges, flats,
pinnaces and shallops plied the rivers. Out over the Bay,
skipjack, ketch and yawl, sloop and schooner, grew in
number so as to rival whitecaps on the waves. They raced
their thoroughbreds and quarterhorses; they hated and
they loved; they argued, quarreled and sometimes moved
away. The watermen dredged for oysters, tonged for
clams, and the soft-shell crab was a regional triumph.
Home-cured ham, pork and pone, turnips and salad
greens, hog jowls and black-eyed peas grew from this
abundant land. And in the evening, when the golden
sunlight of autumn flushed salt meadows and a hundred
thousand wings wheeled in the air and began to settle in,
their appetites were whetted by the splendor of the geese.

America was settled by a world from overseas that cut
down what it found, and then moved on. Fire and ax
destroyed the primal trees. Tobacco robbed the soil of its
fertility, and the exhausted fields were abandoned to the
wind and rain.

Erosion sent the topsoil down the Susquehanna, the
Rappahanock, the Potomac and the James. For every
mile, each year, hundreds of tons of sediment went into
the Bay, and the Chesapeake began to age before its time.

Far out, the sanderlings skim across the headlands and
the beaches, and wheel above the criss-crossed, tumbling
green waters, as the spokes of the sun's wheel strike
through running clouds.

A yellowlegs, turning on itself, yanking through the
shallows, whips out its piercing whistle, and the gulls with
their shivering, silvery screams and laughter, cry out for
water's magical locations.

Backed by the continent, fed by its rivers, entered by
the majesty of the sea, the Bay still speaks a language
of capacity, of endless patience, but it will never endure
a race that only knows how to spend earth's substance on
a world of waste and greed.

Water is birth and mystery,
water in our hearts and minds,
the engines of love and deliberation.
Water is our guide,
however far we turn away.

America meant "improvement." Rivers were channeled,
dammed, bridged over, made useful for navigation.
We did not want them to stand in our way, with their
own rules. We did not like them to run free, leaving us at
the mercy of their floods and periods of low water,
refusing us passage. We improved them, and left them
behind. We loaded their timeless journeys with the deadly
passage of our wastes.

"The rivers of Virginia are the God-given sewers
of the State."
Thus spoke the nineteenth century.
Long live convenience.
God save Virginia.

The germinative rivers, the bringers of life, began to
carry more black oil and poisons to the Bay. The silver
alewives and the shad, mounting the rivers in their
spawning fire, were blocked by dams and started to
disappear. The famous sturgeon was nowhere to be
found. Marsh plants began to die; underwater vegetation
died; numberless oysters never reached maturity. What
has happened to the rockfish, the great striped bass that
spawns in the prolific waters of the Chesapeake, the pride
of all the states that border on the sea? Why is its
progeny being cheated of existence?

The eye of the Chesapeake is clouded over. While the
rivers send their foul discharge into its heart and lungs,
our own senses fail. Water is light and vision. Without its
clarity we soon go blind.

What lies under these pulsing, ribbony waves? Billions of
gallons of industrial waste, a desolation of herbicides and
pesticides, sulphates and nitrates, chlorine, gas and oil.
What lies there but a wasting of the heart?

Only man can destroy the Bay; only man can destroy
himself.

We are the victims of our own ignorance and love of
power. We do not know the limits of these waters, until
we pass them; and we never gave ourselves the time.

Native Americans declared: "A frog does not drink up the
pond in which it lives."

That suggests a frog's intelligence may be on a higher
level than our own. But there is time, within the earth,
for recognition.

Still and always, the seabird lifts to the impenetrable
light that dances on the tides—
And the eyes of schooling fishes stare ahead into the
waterways of the future.

These are true inheritors, children of amplitude, as it
was in the beginning. They live at home with mystery,
the great design of life, in which all species are kindred.
We cannot live outside them and survive.

Until we learn to recognize these waters in ourselves, they
will age, sicken and die. Violence will be returned for
violence, dying for dying. The rivers will turn against us;
the Chesapeake will have its vengeance; the continent will
call us aliens, strangers to its spirit. When the great
network of living veins and arteries begins to shrivel and
dry, the spirit of the people dies. The seas within us die.

America is not the product of industry but of shared
existence.

To give up on the Chesapeake is to give up on ourselves.
Listen to it. Watch its cosmic, universal eye. Rediscover
sanity. Return. Come home again. Come home.

Grass

The wind grew stronger, whisked under stones, carried up straws and old leaves, and even little clods, marking its course as it sailed across the fields. The air and the sky darkened and through them the sun shone redly, and there was a raw sting in the air. During a night the wind raced faster over the land, dug cunningly among the rootlets of the corn, and the corn fought the wind with its weakened leaves until the roots were freed by the prying wind and then each stalk settled wearily sideways toward the earth and pointed the direction of the wind.

The dawn came, but no day. In the gray sky a red sun appeared, a dim red circle that gave a little light, like dusk; and as that day advanced, the dusk slipped back toward darkness, and the wind cried and whimpered over the fallen corn.

John Steinbeck, *The Grapes of Wrath*

I knew grass as a boy because, except in the city, it was always present, everywhere I looked. At the same time, it was unidentifiable, except as hay, or as the grass stems I chewed on to pass the time of day. I knew that if I put my thumbs together, with a grass blade between them, and blew through them I could produce a rasping whistle. On the great pasture beyond my maternal grandparents' house I could watch hay being tossed by the pitchfork and loaded into wagons drawn by patient farm horses. In the barn I could smell the sweet smell of hay while listening to the horses lightly stomping in their stalls. The cows, the great eating factories of our world, did nothing all day long but chew their cud, which struck me as an abysmal way to spend one's life.

I saw other grasses being winnowed by the wind in the salt marshes or on the dunes, tracing compasses in the sand. I watched birds weaving grass into their nests. In the more prosperous parts of the country, grasses meant hay fields, golf courses, and lawns. Otherwise, they only meant the greater wildness of plains, mountains, and deserts which were beyond my reach. It was only in later years, when distinctions became more vital to me, that I began to tell some grasses apart by name.

"What is the grass?" a child asked America's capacious poet, Walt Whitman. "I guess," he answered, "it must be the flag of my disposition, out of hopeful green stuff woven." He equated grass with "the common air that bathes the globe." No more hopeful statement has since been made about the great reaches of a new world.

Yet when land became more and more restricted, exuberance began to dim. Even before land, of course, it was gold, the perpetual pot at the end of the rainbow, that made men blind and merciless in their desire.

In October of 1835, one Captain Thomas Aikens led a party into the mountains of western Colorado. As he reported it: ". . . with my field glasses I could see that the mountains looked right for gold, could see bands of Indian ponies and bands of deer and antelopes grazing close up to the high foothills. Could see that the valley was the loveliest of all the valleys in the scope of my vision. The boys said it will not be safe to venture up until spring, on account of the snow slides.

"But the following morning was so fair, and the love of adventure and hope of gold so inviting, that we forded the Platte and travelled up with the bold mountains all before us, till we pitched our tents under the red rock cliff, at the mouth of Boulder Canyon."

There is a sign at Clear Creek Canyon, at the site of the now abandoned gold mines, with the blasted and scoured hills all around them, that reads: "This creek saw the first great gold discoveries which converted Colorado from a wilderness to a commonwealth."

Captain Aikens's aesthetic sense had helped to lead America from wilderness to industry and "improvement" in record time, and we have been following him ever since.

As the horde of miners kept coming on, Left Hand, an Arapaho chief, said, "Go away, you come to kill our game, to burn our wood, and to destroy our grass." Six years later, Black Kettle, chief of the Cheyenne, sang his death song, as his people were being killed around him: "Nothing lives long, except the earth and the mountains."

A restless, migratory people, pouring in from everywhere, did not have the time to sustain a dialogue with the mountains. Accelerating growth, more violent in its momentum than accommodating, left the ancient signals of wild space behind it.

In the late 1930s, a college classmate and I left my family's house in New Hampshire and drove north in his old Chevy to visit his father, an engineer who worked at a copper and silver mine in Canada. As we began to get close to the mine, we saw a ravaged land, on a scale I had never seen before. The vegetation had been killed for many miles by sulfur fumes from the mine's smokestacks. The only equivalent for it in my limited experience came from images of World War I, with its vast, dark, and burned battlefields, black pits illuminated by incessant bombardment and arching flares, a man-created hell.

These were the drought-ridden, Dust Bowl years. As we drove south again into the northern reaches of the Great Plains, we saw a land, once rich with waving grasses, that had been reduced to a desert. Massive amounts of topsoil had turned to dust and blown away. Clouds of it were seen as far as the eastern seaboard. In North Dakota, the corn had not grown much higher than the stubble to which it is reduced after the harvest. I remember a big, muddy puddle in one farmyard, circled around by a few cows and horses drinking what little water they could get from it.

Farmhouses stood empty across the Great Plains. Perhaps as many as two million farmers had left the impoverished land, piled their possessions into old trucks, Model T Fords, and wagons drawn by horse or by hand, and had moved slowly away from the ravaged land on the dusty road to California. In an eloquent poem about that period called "Land of the Free," Archibald MacLeish wrote:

Worked out corn fields where the soil has left us
Silent and secret: coloring little streams:
Riling in yellow runnels after rainfall:
Dribbling from furrow down into furrow and down into
Fields fallow with winter and on down—
Falling away to the rivers and on down

Taking the life with it
Taking the bread with it:
                              taking a good man's pride in a
Clean field well tilled: his children
Fed from furrows his own plow has made them.

They had earlier migrated out of the eastern forests and their singing glades, their deep hollows and flowering trees, and had looked westward over a great mountain ridge to see the promise of rich lands stretching out ahead of them. There was always something to leave or break out of in America. The true grit, try try again pioneers hacked, cleared, burned their way through nearly impenetrable forests, forded rivers and swamps, until they reached that bountiful prairie land where they could dig in and prosper. The farther west they went, the drier it became, but they hardly noticed that for the great expanse of waving green.

Many early settlers were astonished and appalled by the vastness that met their eyes. Lauren Brown, in her 1979 book *Grasses*, quotes a traveler, who wrote in 1824, "I do not know of anything that struck me more forcibly than the sense of solitude in crossing this, and some other large Prairies. I was perfectly alone, and could see nothing in any direction but sky and grass. Not a living thing could I see or hear, except the occasional rising of some prairie fowl or perhaps a large hawk or eagle wheeling about over my head." In the early part of the nineteenth century, the Great Plains were known as the Western Desert. The rolling prairie probably reminded many immigrants of the trackless, leaden wastes of the Atlantic over which they had traveled to reach America. In spite of an appreciation, partly nostalgic at present, for the "great open spaces," Americans have consistently shown a passionate interest in occupying them and getting rid of the solitude. The great prairie company of plants and animals have not been well served as a result.

Not everyone, of course, saw only hundreds of miles of empty desert ahead of them. An early traveler on the prairies, the artist George Catlin, often praised the beauty of this country in his book *Letters and Notes on the Manners, Customs and Condition of the North American Indians*, which related his travels among them between 1832 and 1839 and described their increasingly beleaguered condition. Writing from an area near "Black Bird's Grave," a bluff along the Missouri River where Blackbird, a famous Omaha chief, was buried, Catlin asserted: "There is no more beautiful prairie country in the world, than that which is to be seen in this vicinity. In looking back from this bluff, towards the West, there is, to an almost boundless extent, one of the most beautiful scenes imaginable. The surface of the country is gracefully and slightly undulating, like the swells of the retiring ocean after a heavy storm. And everywhere covered with a beautiful green turf, and with occasional patches and clusters of trees."

In the region Catlin explored, the grasses grew tall enough to hide Indians on horseback. Again in *North American Indians*, and writing from the vicinity of Fort Leavenworth, in what Catlin called the "Lower Missouri," he describes fires which were one of the great seasonal spectacles of the prairie: "There are many modes by which the fire is communicated to them, both by white men and Indians — *par accident*; and yet many more where it is voluntarily done for the purpose of getting a fresh crop of grass, for the grazing of their horses, and also for easier travelling during the

next summer, when there will be no old grass to lie upon
the prairies, entangling the feet of man and horse, as they
are passing over them."

Catlin describes innumerable prairie chickens, which he
compared to the English grouse, as they were escaping the
wind-driven fire:

> Seeing the prairies on fire several miles ahead of us, and the
> wind driving the fire gradually towards us, we found these
> poor birds driven before its long line, which seemed to extend
> from horizon to horizon, and they were flying in swarms of
> flocks that would at times almost fill the air. . . .
>
> Over the elevated lands and prairie bluffs, where the grass
> is thin and short, the fire slowly creeps with a feeble flame,
> which one can easily step over; where the wild animals often
> rest in their lairs until the flames almost burn their noses,
> when they will reluctantly rise, and leap over it, and trot off
> amongst the cinders, where the fire has passed and left the
> ground as black as jet. These scenes at night become inde-
> scribably beautiful, when their flames are seen at many miles
> distance, creeping over the sides and tops of the bluffs, ap-
> pearing to be sparkling and brilliant chains of liquid fire (the
> hills being lost to the view), hanging suspended in graceful
> festoons from the skies.
>
> But there is yet another character of burning prairies . . .
> the war, or hell of fires! where the grass is seven or eight feet
> high, as is often the case for many miles together, on the Mis-
> souri bottoms; and the flames are driven forward by the hur-
> ricanes, which often sweep over the vast prairies of this de-
> nuded country. There are many of these meadows on the
> Missouri, the Platte, and the Arkansas, of many miles in
> breadth, which are perfectly level, with a waving grass, so high
> that we are obliged to stand erect in our stirrups, in order to
> look over its waving tops as we are riding through it. The fire

in these, before such a wind, travels at an immense and fright-
ful rate, and often destroys, on their fleetest horses, parties of
Indians, who are so unlucky as to be overtaken by it. . . .

. . . Soon after we entered [the high grass], my Indian
guide dismounted slowly from his horse, and lying prostrate
on the ground, with his face in the dirt, he *cried*, and was talk-
ing to the Spirits of the brave — "For," said he, "over this
beautiful plain dwells the Spirit of fire! He rides in yonder
cloud — his face blackens with rage at the sound of the tram-
pling hoofs — the *fire-bow* is in his hand — he draws it across
the path of the Indian, and quicker than lightning, a thousand
flames rise to destroy him; such is the talk of my fathers, and
the ground is whitened with their bones. . . . It is here, also,
that the fleet-bounding wild horse mingles his bones with the
red man; and the eagle's wing is melted as he darts over its
surface. Friends! it is the season of fire; and I fear, from the
smell of the wind, that the Spirit is awake!

The new occupants of the prairie were descended from
rural societies dependent on farm animals, oxen, horses,
sheep, and cows for their livelihood, and they counted on
temperate climates to grow their crops. They may have had
images of biblical fire and flood in their heads, but what was
to come in the aridity of the Great Plains was not in their
experience. At first, the thick sod resisted their efforts to
plow it with the oxen and farm equipment they had brought
with them. Then more advanced, steel plows were introduced, and these set to work to break the plains.

The wild drought- and fire-resistant grasses had exten-
sive root systems twined together for a thousand miles and
reaching into the dark soil they had made over uncounted
millennia. The tall grass prairie's dominant grass was the Big
Bluestem, *Andropogon gairardi*, or Turkey Claw, growing up

to five feet or more, but a major part of it was hidden underground. As William Least Heat Moon describes it in his book *PrairyErth*: ". . . the tall grasses seem to treat the world of sunlight as alien and dangerous, a world to enter as a spinster does the stock market, venturing only a portion at a time on a few blue chippers, yet ready if they fail to cut her losses and get out."

The determined tenant farmers of the 1930s suddenly found themselves cast out, in tragic bewilderment. In a relatively short time, they had subdued a large part of the continent without being aware of the consequences. They never had the time to accommodate the land they came to. They dispossessed it, and so dispossessed themselves. Sun's Pasture, as Archibald MacLeish called it, was replaced with a denuded landscape. (A mightier progress followed to claim the territory again, with massive crops and great machines, backed by political power and subsidies. But the land obeys a more lasting weather.)

Defeated by a fiery drought and by soil that was too far gone to produce an ear of corn, the farmers were tossed out on the public highway, with dust in their throats. They had told themselves that the land was theirs to do with as they pleased, part of the liberty guaranteed them by the Bill of Rights and the Constitution. But now? Many stared out from what was left of their leaning porches, the blind windows facing a desolate horizon, saying, as Archibald MacLeish has it in "Land of the Free":

> We wonder if the liberty was land and the
> Land's gone: the liberty's back of us. . . .
> We can't say,
> We don't know

At present, deep in the numbers game, we count a hundred million years as if they were but a footnote to time, but fail to find them in ourselves. We have become too accustomed to leaving original worlds behind us. The sea of grass, flowering, firing, reflecting the light, known to deep ground, was also known in its inhabitants: coyote, buffalo, antelope, eagle, prairie chicken, prairie dog. They traveled and grew, lived and died, within the body of that sea.

Much of settled New England was deserted during the latter part of the nineteenth century by farm boys lured by the rich, black soil of the prairie states. I remember country roads in New Hampshire which led past cellar holes with rock foundations, and dark, weathered barns not yet fallen under loads of snow. There were still reminders in those granite hills of a Puritan-inspired darkness of spirit not yet dislodged by the larger world outside them. Old people, who had long since been left behind, rocking on their front porches, would look at passersby with the hard unsmiling faces of a generation for whom a lifetime of toil had only led to abandonment. Occasionally, as you approached a house, the scared, white faces of malnourished children would peer out from behind a window.

The headstones of many small, grass-covered cemeteries, away from the new roads and town centers, still trace the history of a hard-won relationship with the land which fell victim to the exodus, especially after the Civil War. Gravestones from the earlier part of the nineteenth century reflect a land of the young. By the last third of the century, the inscriptions record a dwindling population of the old.

What is left of grass-grown, narrow country roads still traces their backbreaking enterprise. Long, often massive, stone walls, rock-lined foundations, deep furrows made by wagons and plows are still there, although the trees that were cut down on a prodigious scale have grown in to claim their own rights, their ancient foothold on the land. Deserted cow pastures have filled in with birch, beech, hemlock, white pine, and maple. The record of the earlier human persistence is still grooved into the ground, but whatever youthful exuberance there might have been is gone into the autumnal glory of the leaves lying out like flags over the land.

"All flesh is grass," said the prophet Isaiah, "and all the goodliness thereof is as the flower of the field.

"The grass withereth, the flower fadeth: because the spirit of the Lord bloweth upon it: surely the people is grass."

But this universal plant, of many colors, the stuff of our disposition, and a measure of infinitude, is now being buried by a crowd anonymity. (Isaiah again: "Woe to the multitude of many people, which make a noise like the noise of the seas: and to the rushing of nations, that make a rushing like the rushing of mighty waters!")

We abhor what we call empty space, simply because we have not yet occupied it. The real estate operators, who are after me to sell part of the dry, wooded acres where we built our house on Cape Cod some forty-five years ago, refer to them as "vacant land." When I first bought it, I was told that it was "worthless woodlot," explaining its low price of twenty-five dollars an acre. The value of the land rose by leaps and bounds following World War II, as a result of the growing appetite of the economy, and a steep rise in population. Its own sparse but individual kind of diversity, which earlier countrymen depended on, was seldom valued as a reason to live there. The idea that we should rarify emptiness as a way of life is so far removed from the earth's realities as to call our assumptions about who and where we are into question. Americans love to win, but we can never win over what we obliterate.

The outcasts of the Dust Bowl years were victims of an almost unconscious experiment in subduing the earth, a right granted them by another high authority, namely the Book of Genesis. But all they had with which to judge their new surroundings was the Old World experience of temperate climates with enough annual rainfall to sustain their crops. The Great Plains could provide them with no more moisture than the drought-resistant grasses and the soil they had built up over the ages could use efficiently.

Just as a lawn or a golf course in desert surroundings will revert to desert unless artificially watered, so the wheat that replaced prairie grasslands requires intensive irrigation. Water is mined from an underground aquifer of inestimable value. Given a future period of prolonged drought, and without the grasses to hold down the soil, there seems to be no reason why it should not blow again.

It has been estimated that the prairie grasses are eighty-two times as effective in conserving soil than are cultivated crops. In H. W. Stasten's *Grasses and Grassland Farming*, published in 1952, it is stated that the top seven inches of soil under corn cultivation would be lost in approximately forty-five years, whereas the grass would hold the soil for more than three thousand; and it would build the soil in the process. A Soil Conservation Experiment Station in Iowa, during the 1930–35 period, found that Kentucky Bluegrass held down the soil so firmly that only 0.3 ton, or 600 pounds, of soil was lost annually, as compared to 246 tons when corn was grown continuously.

We have now lost, and are still losing, a major proportion of our native grasslands and the rich soil they maintained. Only patches of the original tall-grass prairie in its easterly ranges, as far as Illinois and Indiana, still remain. Four million acres of prairie are also conserved in the Flint Hills of Kansas. Farther west, in mid-continent, is the wheat belt that replaced the mixed-grass prairie of the Great Plains, which merges with the semi-arid, short-grass prairie, now used primarily for grazing.

The Land Institute of Salinas, Kansas, estimates that three billion tons of topsoil wash and blow away each year in the United States; and the wheat fields of Kansas and the corn fields of Iowa routinely lose up to two bushels of soil for every bushel of grain produced. The number of people living and working on farms in the United States has declined from thirty million in 1940 to fewer than six million today.

In the words of Wes Jackson, of the Land Institute, "Soils have stayed put for a long time, independent of human action. With the wheat fields come pesticides, fertilizer, fossil energy, and soil erosion. The prairie counts on species diversity, and genetic diversity within species, to avoid epidemics of insects and pathogens. The prairie supports its own fertility."

It is in the profound collaboration of plants, soil, and the elemental powers that life and health are nurtured. The prairie grasses, like the forest trees, are guarantors, in their great containment, of richness and variety. When they are burned, uprooted, and cleared out, the earth is readily invaded by sterility and disease. A shallow-rooted, extractive society leaves the future to chance and impermanence.

As the Arapaho chief predicted, the white man came to

destroy the grass. Some 250 million acres of land were replaced by the self-justified works of man. The length of time it took for uprooted migrants to conquer North America was surprisingly short; we had left half of creation behind us before we had a chance to know it. How much mastery can we claim over nature while deserting it at the same time, heading off into exterior space at an accelerating rate of speed, and with a growing sense of anxiety? What can speed teach us except how to run away from each other, and from the land itself?

Along with our ruinous appetite for plunder, we are becoming hands-off participants in some disengaged machinery. We know the world not because it has always been in us to know, but through manufactured substitutes for reality, vanishing acts which turn us into distant conjurors. But detached, mass methods of dealing with the earth lead to a loss of that significant detail which is the essence of diversity. The enduring nature and spirit of a place is not in single crops but in singular identities, products of timeless adjustments to planetary change. The Sun-Creator and the rain call forth the grass, once regenerated by the Spirit of Fire.

When we first moved to our windy "Dry Hill" above the shore, I was not aware that I had prairie grasses growing only a few yards from our house. Then I still thought grasses were indistinguishable one from another, and was only vaguely aware that they were flowering plants. I knew they covered the earth with various shades of green, but gave them little credit for a detailed mastery of it.

Eventually, living in one place long enough helped me to free the grasses from the tyranny of sameness that I had imposed on them. And there, looking like nothing else, was

Little Bluestem, or prairie beardgrass, *Andropogon scoparius*. The Little Bluestem was once the most abundant of all the grasses growing in the mixed-grass prairie regions; it is now an "old field invader." It is not little, growing to a height of five feet, but it is a slim-shafted plant, the stems and grasses growing close to the stalk. It cannot really be described as blue, although the new growth of shoots in the spring are a bluish-green. Its stalks survive throughout the winter, with colors of dusky red, yellow, or gold, deepening to bronze. Little Bluestem's spent seedheads last well into the autumn months, as little, frost-white pointed tufts that catch the light in all kinds of weather. The individual grasses, growing in clumps, look like feathered lances, or wands summoning the powers of wind, sun, and rain to their aid. This is not just a remnant of species, which we might think of with some nostalgia, as we do the vanished grass-lands of the west, but a survivor of distinction, and an indicator of the nature of the ground in which it grows. (A similar species, with which Little Bluestem is easily confused, is Broom Sedge, *Andropogon virginious*, found in dry fields, or by a railroad track. It grows where fertility is almost gone. You can be sure that any area that supports it has lost its soil.)

The native grasses of America serve a far more fundamental purpose than do the sterile expanses of lawns and golf courses that cover the country. They are under the control of a great and varied continent, as rhythmic as the seas. They can lead you to the true, underlying nature of the ground in which you find yourself.

Fire in the Plants

On this transient existence, you never know whether the person you just met might be the one to whom you have said good-bye. One morning when I was a boy in New Hampshire, my father and I stopped by to have a brief chat with Mr. Rowe, an elderly man who lived up the road from our place. As we talked with him he was leaning over the pasture fence in front of his house, which stood at the foot of Sunset Hill. The very next morning we heard that he had died. For some reason, that meeting made a profound impression on me. Old man Rowe did not have much to say, "keeping to himself," as did others in the neighborhood, but later on, I felt as if I had been present at a significant crossroads in local history. That meeting still hangs in my mind like the imperishable falling of golden leaves.

Our home territory, which was being discovered and inhabited by summer people, was the woods and shore of a major lake that was traversed by steamboat for the sightseers and yet was still defined more by its ancient rocks and forest trees than by any conquering "improvement." The house was built on a rocky slope above the lake, and my boyhood was punctuated with the sound of dynamite, as the interminable boulders were blown up for the sake of lawns and gardens. In spite of local scattered farms and fields, the forests still commanded the landscape, and reached like waves over the mountains and out of sight.

We lived in a cultivated clearing, while clearing out on a major scale was occupying much of the rest of America. I was brought up in an atmosphere of order and civility which many people in contemporary society might find highly cramping to the modern style of uninhibited expression. I have long felt that my parents' generation was haunted by the dark weight of World War I, and by the possibility of another one, gathering before them. I confess that there were times when post-Victorian restraint aroused feelings of rebellion in me, and I was tempted to think that I might break away and hop aboard a freight train heading west. My temerity was never tested. I was kept from the open road by the advent of World War II, when I was drafted into the army.

My grandfather had bought his land in New Hampshire from local farmers in the last decade of the nineteenth century, at a time when many farms were being abandoned. The Lake Sunapee area was not a resort on anything like the scale of Bar Harbor, or Newport, Rhode Island. There was one large hotel, and lodging houses only a few miles away. My grandparents' house, enlarged as the years went by, occupied what was essentially a clearing on a hill leading down to the lake. Before he was married, my father had a log cabin on the place where he used to stay during off seasons, hiking and fishing. Some years after inheriting the main house, with the aid of skilled Italian masons who had settled in the area, he started construction of a rock garden that extended down the rocky slope below the house. It was a Herculean task, this "gardening in granite," as he called it, but watching the plants over the years, on his return from work as an archaeologist in New York and Mexico, was a great source of pleasure to him.

My father loved gardens, no less than did my mother, whose main interest was in roses and flower beds. As a result of her childhood experience at the old family farm in Ipswich, where "the great pasture" was meant for livestock rather than trees, New Hampshire's wild trees and the untended parts of its landscape were not altogether to her liking. It was the resistant part of the land she found hard to tolerate. My parents' attitudes represented two different, if not irreconcilable, views toward a stubborn land that still retained much of the character of a wilderness.

Mother had some decided ideas about flower beds, roses in particular. To her, I think, roses were a symbol of civilization, lifting their lovely heads above the unruly disorder of the outside world. She would tolerate no intruders in the rose beds. Mice, as well as the moles that made humpbacked trails across the lawn, were unacceptable. Weeds were torn out on arrival, as were forest seedlings, which were everywhere. My mother's efforts to cultivate roses were annually frustrated by the realities of New Hampshire. At least half of them were "winter killed" and had to be replaced, a fact that did not stop my mother for a moment.

She had a deep-seated antipathy for snakes, which had biblical authority behind it, and her attitude toward other intruders such as the insects that attacked us or invaded the flowers was unflinching. With a natural perversity of my own, I once introduced a garter snake into the house, to educate her, I suppose, and her response was almost terrifying. Mother had a strong vein of the "practical" in her, which she applied to all unnecessary flights of the imagination. I told her that I believed in flying saucers, and one year I actually saw one spinning in the sky, or so I thought. Wasting no time in rescuing me from my delusions, she phoned the weather bureau, which identified the object as one of their high-flying instruments. It was never easy to detect the chinks in her armor, although like the rest of us she had unspoken fears she did not find it easy to admit. Wilderness was a concept she was unable to understand, but she took courage from inherited ideas of order and behavior, as did my father. Even so, in a country with a relatively small population by comparison with today, and a wealth of space, they never overpowered the natural world around them, but accommodated it. A wilder space, visible and invisible, governed our lives. That, I know, was the reason why a greener condition in a lawn free of weeds did not interest me half as much as a deeper, still undiscovered meaning in the trees, where I might hear an owl, or walk through drifting snow.

After having to move away from our house in New Hampshire, dislodged by circumstance and the plunging moods of my times, I still returned on many occasions to pursue a silent dialogue with the trees. I hear in them a condition that parallels my own. In their successional stages of growth, pines, maples, beech, and canoe birches seem to embody a shared time created out of a permanence that defies us. There is a hemlock that I have faced since my year one. It stands on the lake side of a cottage we used to stay in during the seasons of spring, autumn, and winter. I hardly noticed the tree as a boy, but it is still there, as if it had patiently waited for me while I was absent for so many years. Its tall, straight reddish-brown trunk looks smooth and youthful, now that I am entering old age. Since hemlocks grow to be four hundred years old or more, it may be still there, growing ahead of me several centuries from now. That tree is a signal for me of imperishable growth. Cut them all down and we would live in a land untenanted by any certainty. Those great trees, growing ahead of and behind me, are my protectors, with their branches gently dipping in the wind, shedding sunlight and snow. They are generators and providers. Why should we refuse their priceless heritage?

The northern trees are travelers, responding to the great age and space of the continent. "Our own native flora," wrote Edgar Anderson in *Plants, Man and Life*, contrasting it with the European, "was bred for our violent American climate. It goes into winter condition with a bang. The leaves wither rapidly, they drop off in a short time, frost or no frost. In their hurry many of them leave enough chemicals behind to give us brilliant fall color. Virtually all the autumnal green which one sees in the eastern and central United States is European."

The hurricane of 1938 left indescribable wreckage behind it, uprooting trees, knocking down wide swathes of white pines by the lake and in exposed clearings. In the woodlands, the evidence can still be seen of rotting trees now becoming part of the leaf mould. But the trees grew back undefeated, competing for space, in a coexistent, tight race for air, soil, and sunlight. Beech, birch, ash, maple, and hemlock have claimed former territories and moved into new ones. I marvel at their vitality and insistence. In their silence, receiving, standing, rather than escaping as we do, creating their own shadows, rebuilding the character of the land, they tell us where we are. They are subject to long or

short cycles of blight and disease. Individual trees are uprooted by strong winds. An isolated pine is hit by lightning
and bears the scar. Some trees, as if in a desperate struggle
to claim their own space, tend to displace or kill each other
off.

I have seen a mountainside covered with dead balsam fir,
killed off by rime and ice driven into the trees' tissues by
winter storms. The seedlings come in thick again to take
their chances within the extremities. The endurance and
hardihood of those trees is worth more than a moment's
reflection. Born of a magnificent, varied, and violent continent, they follow its lead without fail. The more we destroy them, the more rootless we become. Whenever I find
myself in the presence of an old white pine, stirring and
creaking like a schooner on the high seas, I honor it for
bringing back the grand dimensions of earth history.

My sister and I were constantly criticized by our father
for the improper use of words. He himself was not an author, as his father had been, but an archaeologist. Never-
theless, he inherited an older tradition of proper usage.
"Bad grammar" was frowned upon in those days. We did
our best to improve, I suppose, without having much sense
of verbal construction, but how to say things correctly
seemed to me to be less important than what was being left
out. What's within a name? Words often tricked me with
double allusions, and names too seemed to hide a wealth of
meaning. It took a more advanced education for me to see
why plants had to have Latin names in an intellectual sense,
but in the meantime they seemed to have lost their lives to
names. I knew garden species by what they were called, as
well as by their look and their scent, but that knowledge
tended to limit me to plants that were considered accept-

able. What were those wretched weeds that were sent packing as soon as they appeared? Nothing, as I learned later, but a whole universe of plant life. I was not aware for a long time that the red trillium, the local name for which was "Stinking Benjamin," which grew in wet places in the spring and had a bad smell, attracted carrion flies, but that may be the reason I was never told about it. It was pretty to look at, but "unattractive" to smell. My private quarrel with the civilizers was that they claimed too much and let in too little. My liberators were always being disguised by the names they were given. Surely, flowering plants, I began to think, were more, said more, than a recital of their component parts.

One evening, in later years, when an amateur pursuit of natural history had led me out into wider and wilder fields than horticulture offered me, I spent an hour or more watching a flower fold up in response to the setting sun. It seemed at the time a miraculous revelation. Where had I been not to realize that flowering plants were working partners of the sun? Why had no one ever suggested such a thing before?

When I felt it was important to me to know what a salt marsh was composed of, I began to learn its distinctions. Every species there was expressing itself in terms of the tidal, rhythmic character of its surroundings. The colors of the salt-tolerant grasses changed with the seasons, from wide patches of blue-green or yellowish-green that looked like the shadows made by traveling clouds, to fall colors of tawny gold. Very early in spring when the new shoots were starting to appear on the surface of the marsh, I looked down at where the spike grass and blank grass grew on the marsh edges. I could see that, at this stage, individual stems and leaves were starting up in clear distinction from each other. There was no undifferentiated emergence in this process of growth. The grasses were forming a scaffolding of intricate design. It is through such minor observations that we begin to take the measure of ourselves.

A society interested only in quick results has little time to spend on the rhythmic responses in a salt marsh or a wood that might be its salvation. At times I think that all the plants, birds, fish, and every other living organism are waiting for our departure so that they can resume timeless engagement with the earth. Since I learned that plant seeds can live in a state of suspended animation for extraordinary lengths of time, I have felt that they must be responding to the inner pulsing of the earth itself. Buried seeds may live in a state of dormancy for widely varying periods, germinating most often when the soil is disturbed and they come to the surface. Experiments have shown that many common agricultural seeds can remain dormant and viable for decades. Seeds of an arctic lupin found in the burrows of lemmings in Canada's Yukon territory were still viable after an estimated ten thousand years. It is thought that they had been buried and insulated in a frozen state by a landslide. It is as if seeds can internalize time in themselves, as part of a strategy of dispersal. Some species that specialize in colonizing open ground can, in effect, wait in a dormant state until the ground is disturbed, with the result that they are more widely dispersed.

Much has been made of nonverbal communication, or "body language," in humans and other animals. It would never occur to most of us that plants "say" anything at all, except in terms of what we read into them, or try to use them for. Yet in their responses to this wonderfully rhythmic and varying earth they are the most expressive of all the forms of life.

The New Hampshire of my youth led me, following Emily Dickinson, to amplitude and awe. The long stone walls never quite ended in a sad and unfinished history, but opened out, like the great American land itself, to endless possibilities. The presence of original space, and not its alteration at human hands, encouraged me, as the years went by, in looking for all the significant detail from which I had been distracted by my times. It was not identification for its own sake that moved me ahead but the alliances it revealed. I began to see the worlds of life as centered in a mystery of light. The distinctive worlds, of birds, fish, mammals, insects, and plants, were never as fixed as our naming tended to make them, but shared in the rhythmic patterns and cadences of the earth and sea. Particulars became of the greatest importance to me, because they led me not only to an understanding of diversity, but also to a brilliance in creation. All the environments I ever visited were not only distinct in themselves but shaded off into the unseen and the unfinished. Human isolation from the rest of life on a scale the modern world has made possible is inadmissible in the rest of nature.

Perhaps because I was used to looking at plants in terms of our manipulation of them, the life of plants once seemed passive to me. I did not credit them with an independent existence. It did not occur to me at first that what is rooted in the earth must share in its powers of integration and expression.

A little further climbing, which always characterized New Hampshire in my mind, led me up its granite slopes with their plates of mica shining in the summer sun. There

I learned to recognize some of the tundra species of plants that hug the cracks and crevices for their sparse nutriment and shelter. Hundreds of thousands of pitiless arctic winters describe this adaptation. They exist not by virtue of their ability to avoid exposure but to embody it. They deserve the name of endurance as much as any early arctic explorer stranded on the ice floes of the Canadian north. There is a power in their fragility. They are residents of the most extreme environments on earth, and all climates in between. A single leaf is a map in outline of their universal travels.

There is a bog not far from where we lived in New Hampshire which is surrounded by hardwoods and evergreens. Only during the past one hundred years its plants have been filling in what was once a pond. In living memory, people have been seen rowing a boat across it. I have gone there a number of times out of fascination for this process of colonization and closing in. In its rhythmic response, though carried out over a longer period of time, it seems like the beat, the systole and diastole, of the human heart. This bog is limited in extent. Because it is highly acidic and low in nutrients, it supports only a limited number of species. Some birds feed on its fringes and a varying amount of insects occupy it in season. It is here that the carnivorous pitcher plant survives, employing some ingenious devices to attract and consume the food it requires.

The leaves of the pitcher plant are goblet- or trumpet-shaped. The flowers are red, borne on single stems, and are cross-pollinated by a fly, whose larvae feed on insects that are trapped by the plant and also ingested by it. These insects, attracted by the plant, or accidentally landing on it, are caught by fine, sticky hairs that line the underside of the leaves. At the bottom they are drowned by rainwater that has collected there.

One fine autumn day I peered into one of the leaves and saw the fine, downward pointing hairs, and the red, almost animal-like veins that ran through their green material. The sunlight turned the leaf into a semi-transparent vase. At its base a small pool of rainwater had collected and there were the drowned bodies of insects floating on the surface. I also glimpsed some glistening larval eggs down there, which were apparently able to survive the coming of frosty weather.

Stealth and deceit are employed by this remarkable plant, to drown the innocent and save the elect. There is no fear or love in it, at least as far as we know them, seizing us unawares. Death is fitted to digestion, and reproduction is carried on the wings of a fly. But in its containment of the grand design, nothing beats it for economy. It leads, by extension, from hell to paradise.

I think I have the silent chemistry in me of the lands in which I grew up. At any season a cool wind often passes across my face. I hear the sound of water, salt or fresh, booming in the distance, or trickling nearby. The brown color of the soil is reflected in the coats of the animals that live there, such as the woodchuck or the deer mouse. Under the leaf litter and between the roots of the trees is a teeming world of ants, centipedes, millipedes, sowbugs, and other nearly invisible creatures thriving in the moist and protected soil. The roots are my own assurance of gravity and holding on. My inner clock circles with the trees as far as the skies that wheel above our house. And I count on an all-pervading greenness to fix the sun. I hold my hand with its own veins and arteries up to the sunlight, and see in it the image of a leaf.

I am something of a stranger to the desert. My trips there have only been of short duration. I was not encircled by trees or bodies of water in that arid land, but taken far out to a range of radiant light and color. And there the plants are expressing, in often spectacular form, their open engagement with the sun. It is as if they consumed the light and at the same time had any number of devices to protect them.

A beginner in the desert, I am not only thinking of how to avoid direct exposure to a sun I am not accustomed to. I also wonder what is called out in the human spirit by such openness. One is shunted from glaring light to the other polar extremity of nightfall dropping like a vast dispensation of mystery for which we have no adequate words. There is great antiquity here, which flies in the face of the modern world's desertion of it. The vast distances of the past have their true integrity and meaning out there. It is fortunate that there are native people who have an unbroken connection with it in their minds. I was told of a Papago in recent years who was looking at a petroglyph on a cliff face in Arizona, and said, "See, my ancestors, still dancing for rainbows."

The giant saguaro cactus, which can grow up to fifty feet in height and weigh twelve tons, has a life span of two hundred years. It has the capacity to store a great amount of water in its spongy tissues. Within four to six hours of a heavy rainfall, it shows a measurable increase in circumference, swelling up like a great bellows. At the same time it sends out thousands of inches of root hairs into the desert soil. Heedless development has destroyed great numbers of these desert giants. Their peril calls to mind the greed that threatens to decimate the African elephants and their magnificent heritage.

Several years ago, I went with Gary Nabhan, botanist and author, on a three-day trip starting from Organ Pipe Cactus National Monument in Arizona. We drove west on the Mexican side of the border through desert country that was like a vast wild garden, as a result of unusually heavy spring rains. Some of the flowering shrubs stood out like great lanterns, attracting scintillating hummingbirds with their blossoms. I learned that the flowers of the desert primrose change color from pink to white, a decoloration that serves as a signal to various kinds of insects that the plant has stopped pollinating, and need not be visited. Other plants I was introduced to were able, through fuzzy, spiny, or thorny surfaces, to reduce solar input, the extreme intensity of the desert light. I saw in a blue Papago lily a color which was as deep and arresting as any grotto in the Mediterranean. Plants hold on to what is typical of them in any given environment, but they also embody any number of varying characteristics. I was starting, in myself, to move in response to a vast range of expression, and I pitied us for all our reductions and evasions in the interests of human domination. Should we not be highly offended at being cut off by a poverty of thought from all the living resources that are open to our hearts and souls?

Gary and I reached the northernmost corner of the Gulf of California, where a beach bordered far-reaching tidelands. Its silty sands were deposited by the once mighty Colorado. I saw a number of shorebirds there, western sandpipers, kittiwakes, bristle-thighed curlews, and a few black brant, a western race of those small geese I love to watch off Massachusetts. The birds are those who carry the sense of the globe's geography, and I go back to them to locate myself on migratory routes we seldom follow. To hear the musical calls of the gulls along another shore is to realize that each distinctive song or call is part of the fluctuating environment from which it rises.

After a meal and beer at a Mexican village just behind the beach, and a few more welcome lessons in desert plants, we headed for a high dune on which we spent the night. The night was beautifully clear and deep, with a sky full of trellised and trailing stars. Each star seemed to me to have its corresponding light in a desert flower.

I woke up to a pale blue sky, and as I looked out across the desert to the east, a brilliant eye appeared over a line of low hills. It was soon followed by the red-orange, yellow, flaming turbulence of the dawn, and it seemed as if all the desert flowers, like fires in themselves, were responding in any number of graduated ways. As the light of a new day flooded over land and sea, I thought of all the awakening and responding of all the lives I could not see. The watchers of the night took to the shadows, as the plants received the sunlight. I could hear a rooster crowing. Then a beat-up old pickup truck with a broken muffler roared out on the main road to the village.

So, out of uncountable years, endless opportunities are opened up again in another rising of the sun, and they belong not to a single species like the human race, but to the universe of life. We are all upgraded by the light, so strictly interpreted by the desert plants. It is in this great poverty shared by every living thing without exception that we are discovered, not as the identifiers only, but as the identified.